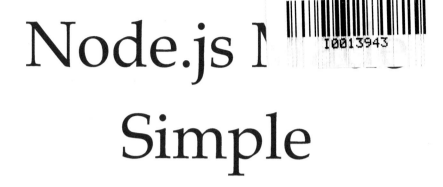

Node.js Made Simple

Hands-On Exercises for Node.js Beginners

By Laurence Lars Svekis

Dedicated to
Alexis and Sebastian
Thank you for your support

For more content and to learn more, visit

https://basescripts.com/

Get the source code at

https://github.com/lsvekis/NodeJS-for-beginners

Introduction

Welcome to **Node.js Made Simple**, a practical guide designed to help you take your first steps into the world of server-side programming with Node.js. This book is crafted with beginners in mind, offering hands-on exercises to help you not only understand the fundamentals of Node.js but also gain the confidence to build real-world applications.

Why This Book?

Node.js is a game-changer in modern web development, empowering developers to build fast, scalable, and efficient server-side applications using JavaScript — the language you likely already know and love. This book is your gateway to mastering the basics of Node.js, with an emphasis on **learning by doing**. Whether you're completely new to back-end programming or you're a front-end developer looking to expand your skill set, this book provides a step-by-step learning experience that ensures you'll walk away with practical skills.

What You'll Learn

In this book, you'll:

- Understand the core concepts of Node.js, including modules, asynchronous programming, and event-driven architecture.
- Learn to build HTTP servers and APIs from scratch.
- Work with essential Node.js modules like `fs` for file handling and `http` for server creation.
- Explore npm (Node Package Manager) to manage dependencies and use third-party libraries effectively.

- Create projects that solve real-world problems, giving you the confidence to tackle your own challenges.
- Debug and troubleshoot common issues, ensuring you develop strong problem-solving skills as you learn.

How to Get the Most Out of This Book

1. **Follow Along with the Exercises:**
   Each chapter is filled with practical exercises that you can code along with. Don't just read — open up your code editor and type the examples yourself. Experiment with them, break them, and try to fix them. That's the best way to learn.
2. **Set Up Your Environment:**
   Ensure you have Node.js installed on your machine before diving in. Instructions for setup are provided early in the book, so you're ready to code from the very first exercise.
3. **Take Your Time with Each Chapter:**
   Each chapter builds upon the previous one. Resist the urge to skip ahead, as the exercises are designed to progressively increase your understanding.
4. **Experiment Beyond the Examples:**
   Once you complete an exercise, challenge yourself by tweaking the code. Add new features, try alternative methods, or explore additional Node.js modules.
5. **Refer to Online Documentation:**
   As you grow more comfortable, use this book as a foundation to explore Node.js's extensive online documentation. Becoming familiar with documentation is an essential skill for any developer.
6. **Ask Questions and Seek Support:**
   If you encounter challenges, don't hesitate to seek help. Join the Node.js community, ask questions on forums

like Stack Overflow, and connect with other learners and developers.

Why Hands-On Learning?

Books that focus solely on theory often leave you wondering how to apply what you've learned. In contrast, this book emphasizes **practical exercises** that bring concepts to life. By the time you finish, you'll have built small yet functional projects that showcase the power of Node.js, giving you the confidence to start your own applications.

Final Thoughts

Node.js is a versatile and exciting platform that's in high demand across the tech industry. By dedicating time to the hands-on exercises in this book, you're taking a big step toward becoming a competent back-end developer.

So, grab your keyboard, set up your development environment, and let's dive into the world of Node.js. Together, we'll take the mystery out of server-side programming and make it simple, fun, and accessible.

Let's get started!

Introduction to Node.js

What is Node.js?

Definition and purpose:
Node.js is an open-source, cross-platform JavaScript runtime environment built on Chrome's V8 JavaScript engine. In simple terms, it allows developers to run JavaScript code outside of a web browser — particularly on the server side. This makes JavaScript a full-stack language that can be used to create both client-side and server-side applications.

Node.js was created to address the limitations of traditional web servers, enabling developers to build fast and scalable network applications. By adopting an event-driven, non-blocking I/O model, Node.js excels at handling numerous simultaneous connections with high throughput.

History and Why It Was Created

A brief history:

- **2009**: Ryan Dahl introduced Node.js. He was inspired by the need to handle a large number of connections concurrently, more efficiently than existing web servers like Apache.
- **V8 Engine**: Node.js uses Google's V8 engine, which compiles JavaScript directly to machine code, giving it impressive performance.
- **Growing Community**: Over the years, an active open-source community has formed around Node.js, creating a massive ecosystem of libraries and tools.

Reason behind its creation:

- **Asynchronous I/O**: Before Node.js, many server-side technologies relied on a multi-threaded model. Node.js was designed to handle I/O asynchronously on a single thread, reducing overhead and increasing efficiency.
- **JavaScript Everywhere**: JavaScript was initially seen as a browser-only language. Node.js effectively changed the landscape by letting developers use JavaScript on the back end, unlocking the potential for "JavaScript everywhere."

Key Features of Node.js

1. **JavaScript Runtime Outside the Browser**
   Node.js frees JavaScript from the confines of the browser. You can build standalone scripts, command-line tools, and fully fledged server-side applications — using a language you already know from client-side development.
2. **Non-Blocking, Event-Driven Architecture**
   - **Event Loop**: At the core of Node.js is an event loop that listens for events and dispatches callbacks.
   - **Non-Blocking I/O**: Operations such as file reads and network requests do not block the main thread. Instead, they use callbacks or Promises/async-await, allowing other tasks to proceed.
3. **Lightweight and Scalable**
   - **Single-Threaded Model**: Node.js runs on a single thread, which reduces overhead from context-switching.
   - **Microservices and APIs**: Node.js is well-suited for creating small, modular microservices that can be scaled horizontally.

Why Learn Node.js?

1. **Popularity in the Industry**
   - **Used by Major Companies**: Organizations like Netflix, PayPal, and LinkedIn rely on Node.js for its performance and scalability.
   - **Vast Ecosystem**: The npm registry is the world's largest software registry, with millions of packages available.
2. **Versatility for Building Server-Side and Full-Stack Applications**
   - **Single Language Across the Stack**: Node.js allows you to use JavaScript on both front end and back end.
   - **Extensive Libraries and Frameworks**: Frameworks like Express.js, NestJS, and Koa simplify building APIs and web applications.

Coding Examples

Below are a few short code snippets to illustrate Node.js usage:

1. **Hello World (Node.js style)**

```
// hello.js
console.log("Hello, World from Node.js!");
```

- **How to run:**
    1. Save the file as `hello.js`.

In your terminal, type:

```
node hello.js
```

    2. You should see `Hello, World from Node.js!` in your console.
2. **Basic HTTP Server**

```js
// server.js
const http = require('http');
// Create a server
const server = http.createServer((req, res)
=> {
  res.writeHead(200, { 'Content-Type':
'text/plain' });
  res.end('Hello, Node.js HTTP Server!');
});
// Listen on port 3000
server.listen(3000, () => {
  console.log('Server is running at
http://localhost:3000/');
});
```

- **Explanation:**
    - We use Node's built-in `http` module to create a server.
    - `createServer` expects a callback function that handles incoming requests (`req`) and outgoing responses (`res`).
    - The server listens on port `3000`, so you can visit `http://localhost:3000` in your browser.
3. **Asynchronous File Read**

```js
// readFile.js
const fs = require('fs');
fs.readFile('example.txt', 'utf8', (err,
data) => {
  if (err) {
    return console.error(err);
  }
  console.log('File content:', data);
});
console.log('This message shows before file
reading completes!');
```

- **Explanation:**
  - `fs.readFile` is an asynchronous operation.
  - While Node.js reads the file in the background, the program continues to the next line (hence, you see `This message shows before file reading completes!` immediately).
  - Once the file read is finished, the callback is executed, logging the file content.

Wrap-Up

You've now been introduced to Node.js — the platform that extended JavaScript's reach to server-side and beyond. You've also seen how Node.js was created to solve specific issues related to scalability and concurrency through a non-blocking, event-driven architecture.

- **Key Takeaways**:
  1. Node.js allows JavaScript to run outside the browser.
  2. Its event-driven, non-blocking I/O model is suited for high-traffic scenarios.
  3. The single-threaded approach can handle many concurrent connections efficiently.
  4. A large community and ecosystem back Node.js, making it popular and versatile.

Use the coding exercises to deepen your understanding of Node.js basics. Test your knowledge with the quiz questions, and keep exploring more advanced features such as modules, package management, and frameworks like Express.js as you progress in your Node.js journey.

Chapter 1. Node.js for Beginners

Setting Up Your Environment and Core Concepts

Since we've already covered what Node.js is, why it was created, and why you might want to learn it, let's move forward to practical aspects of using Node.js. In this section, we'll discuss how to set up your development environment, how to use Node's built-in tools (like the REPL), and how to manage packages effectively. We'll also look at core concepts you'll need day-to-day, such as module exports and ES modules. Along the way, you'll find a variety of exercises and quiz questions to deepen your understanding.

1. Installing and Managing Node.js

1.1. Downloading and Installing Node.js

The simplest way to install Node.js on Windows, macOS, or Linux is to go to the official Node.js website and download the installer for your operating system. Typically, you have two versions to pick from:

- **LTS (Long-Term Support)**: More stable, recommended for most users.
- **Current**: Has the latest features but may change more rapidly.

1.2. Using a Version Manager (Optional but Recommended)

If you want to switch between Node.js versions easily, consider using a version manager:

- **nvm (Node Version Manager)** on macOS/Linux.
- **nvm-windows** or **fnm** on Windows.

With these tools, you can install multiple Node.js versions and switch with a single command (e.g., `nvm use 14`, `nvm use 16`, etc.).

2. Node.js REPL

REPL stands for **Read-Eval-Print Loop**, an interactive shell where you can type JavaScript commands and see results instantly.

Launch the REPL: Open your terminal (or command prompt) and type:

```
node
```

- **Exit the REPL**: Press `Ctrl + C` twice or type `.exit`.

Example: Testing a Simple Math Operation in REPL

```
$ node
Welcome to Node.js v16.x.x.
Type ".help" for more information.
> 2 + 2
4
> .exit
```

This quick test can be handy when you want to verify a snippet of JavaScript logic without creating a file.

3. Working with Modules

In Node.js, you can break your application into separate files and modules to keep your code organized. Node.js supports:

- **CommonJS Modules** (using `require` and `module.exports`)
- **ES Modules** (using `import` and `export`)

3.1. CommonJS Example

```js
// mathUtils.js
function add(a, b) {
  return a + b;
}
function multiply(a, b) {
  return a * b;
}
// Export multiple functions
module.exports = {
  add,
  multiply
};
// main.js
const mathUtils = require('./mathUtils'); // or './mathUtils.js'
console.log(mathUtils.add(2, 3));        // Output: 5
console.log(mathUtils.multiply(2, 3));   // Output: 6
```

3.2. ES Module Example

```js
// mathUtils.mjs
export function subtract(a, b) {
  return a - b;
```

```
}
export function divide(a, b) {
  return a / b;
}
// main.mjs
import { subtract, divide } from
'./mathUtils.mjs';
console.log(subtract(10, 3)); // Output: 7
console.log(divide(10, 2));   // Output: 5
```

Note: Using ES modules may require adding "type":
"module" in your package.json or using the .mjs file
extension.

4. Package Management with npm and package.json

4.1. Initializing a Node Project

Create a new folder for your project:

```
mkdir my-first-project
cd my-first-project
```
Initialize a package.json file:

```
npm init -y
```

1. This creates a basic package.json with default
   values.

4.2. Installing Packages

Local installation: Installs a package into your project's
node_modules folder.

```
npm install lodash
```

Global installation: Installs packages system-wide (less common for app dependencies, more common for CLI tools).

```
npm install -g nodemon
```

Your `package.json` will be updated automatically with any locally installed package under `"dependencies"`.

5. Configuration Files and Scripts

5.1. Using Scripts in package.json

You can define custom commands under the `scripts` section. For example:

```
{
  "name": "my-first-project",
  "version": "1.0.0",
  "scripts": {
    "start": "node main.js",
    "test": "echo \"Running tests...\" &&
exit 0"
  }
}
```

- **Run the script**: `npm run start`
- **Run the test script**: `npm run test`

10 Coding Exercises

Below are ten hands-on exercises with full code, learning objectives, outcomes, and detailed explanations to help you practice the fundamentals of Node.js setup, modules, and package management.

Exercise 1: Check Your Node.js Version

Learning Objective: Familiarize yourself with the Node.js command line and version checking.

1. **Create a script** named `versionCheck.js`.

Code:

```
// versionCheck.js
console.log("Your Node.js version is:",
process.version);
```

How to run:

```
node versionCheck.js
```

2. **Expected Outcome**:
   You'll see something like `Your Node.js version is: v22.11.0` in your terminal.

Explanation:
This exercise demonstrates how to run a Node.js script and use the `process.version` property to fetch your current Node.js version. It also confirms that your environment is set up correctly.

Exercise 2: Using the REPL for Quick Tests

Learning Objective: Gain proficiency in using the Node.js REPL interactively.

1. **Open your terminal** and type `node`.

Perform a few tasks:

```
> let greeting = "Hello from the REPL!";
> greeting
> function double(x) { return x * 2; }
```

```
> double(5)
```

2. **Observe**:
   - o The REPL immediately evaluates expressions.
   - o You can define variables and functions on the fly.
3. **Exit** by typing `.exit` or pressing `Ctrl + C` twice.

Outcome:
You will understand how to test snippets of JavaScript quickly, without writing a full `.js` file.

Exercise 3: Creating a Simple Local Module

Learning Objective: Understand how to create and import a local CommonJS module.

1. **Create two files**: `stringUtils.js` and `app.js`.

stringUtils.js:

```
// stringUtils.js
function toUpperCase(str) {
   return str.toUpperCase();
}
module.exports = {
   toUpperCase
};
```

app.js:

```
// app.js
const { toUpperCase } =
require('./stringUtils');
const phrase = "hello node.js modules";
console.log(toUpperCase(phrase));
```

Run:

```
node app.js
```

2. **Outcome**:
   It will print HELLO NODE.JS MODULES to the console.

Explanation:
This solidifies your understanding of the CommonJS module system, showing how to separate code into different files for better organization.

Exercise 4: Creating an ES Module

Learning Objective: Practice using ES modules (import/export) in Node.js.

1. **Create two files**: mathESM.mjs and index.mjs.

mathESM.mjs:

```
// mathESM.mjs
export function square(x) {
  return x * x;
}
export function cube(x) {
  return x * x * x;
}
```

index.mjs:

```
// index.mjs
import { square, cube } from './mathESM.mjs';
console.log("Square of 4:", square(4));
console.log("Cube of 3:", cube(3));
```

2. **Add "type": "module"** in your package.json, or use the .mjs extension as shown.

Run:

```
node index.mjs
```

Outcome:

```
Square of 4: 16
Cube of 3: 27
```

Explanation:
ES Modules provide an official standardized way to import/export code. This differs from CommonJS primarily in syntax and usage but can coexist in Node.js projects depending on configuration.

Exercise 5: Initializing a package.json and Installing a Package

Learning Objective: Learn how to create a Node.js project and manage dependencies.

In a new folder, run:

```
npm init -y
```

Install a package (e.g., Lodash):

```
npm install lodash
```

Create a file named testLodash.js:

```
// testLodash.js
const _ = require('lodash');
const numbers = [1, 2, 3, 4, 5];
const shuffled = _.shuffle(numbers);
console.log("Shuffled array:", shuffled);
```

Run:

```
node testLodash.js
```

1. **Outcome**:
    The console shows a randomized version of
    [1,2,3,4,5].

Explanation:
You'll see how `package.json` automatically tracks installed dependencies, and you'll learn how to use them in your code with `require`.

Exercise 6: Global vs. Local Installation

Learning Objective: Understand the difference between globally and locally installed packages.

Globally install a simple CLI tool, like `http-server`:

```
npm install -g http-server
```
Confirm installation:

```
http-server --version
```
Run the server:

```
# Start a server in the current directory
http-server
```

1. **Outcome**:
    You can access `http://localhost:8080` to see the directory listing.

Explanation:
Globally installed packages become available system-wide, typically used for command-line tools. Locally installed packages reside in `node_modules` within your project directory and are used specifically by that project.

Exercise 7: Creating and Running a Custom Script in package.json

Learning Objective: Learn how to define and use npm scripts to streamline development.

Create a `start.js` file:

```
// start.js
console.log("Running my custom start
script!");
```

Add a script in `package.json`:

```
{
  "name": "my-app",
  "version": "1.0.0",
  "scripts": {
    "start": "node start.js"
  }
}
```

Run the script:

```
npm run start
```

1. **Outcome**:
   You'll see `Running my custom start script!` in the console.

Explanation:
Defining custom npm scripts helps you avoid typing long commands. You can also chain commands (e.g., building your project, running tests, etc.).

Exercise 8: Using require for Built-in Modules

Learning Objective: Learn to use Node.js core modules without installing anything additional.

Create a file `osInfo.js`:

```
// osInfo.js
const os = require('os');
console.log("Platform:", os.platform());
console.log("CPU Architecture:", os.arch());
console.log("Total Memory:", os.totalmem());
console.log("Free Memory:", os.freemem());
console.log("Home Directory:", os.homedir());
```
Run:

```
node osInfo.js
```

1. **Outcome:**
   You'll see details about your operating system in the console.

Explanation:
Node.js provides numerous built-in modules (like `os`, `http`, `fs`) for system-level operations. No need to install them—they're included by default.

Exercise 9: Simple CLI Input

Learning Objective: Practice reading command-line arguments with `process.argv`.

Create `cliGreetings.js`:

```
// cliGreetings.js
const args = process.argv.slice(2); // skip
first two default entries
const name = args[0] || "Stranger";
console.log(`Hello, ${name}!`);
```

Run:

```
node cliGreetings.js John
```

1. **Outcome**:
   You'll see `Hello, John!` in the console. If you run
   without arguments, you get `Hello, Stranger!`.

Explanation:
`process.argv` contains everything typed on the command
line: the Node executable path, the script path, and then user-
provided arguments.

Exercise 10: Combining Exports from Multiple Modules

Learning Objective: Understand modular organization by
combining exports from different files into one aggregator
module.

1. **Create three files**: `uppercase.js`, `lowercase.js`,
   `stringIndex.js`.

uppercase.js:

```
// uppercase.js
function uppercase(str) {
   return str.toUpperCase();
}
module.exports = uppercase;
```
lowercase.js:

```
// lowercase.js
function lowercase(str) {
   return str.toLowerCase();
}
module.exports = lowercase;
```

stringIndex.js:

```
// stringIndex.js
const uppercase = require('./uppercase');
const lowercase = require('./lowercase');
module.exports = {
  uppercase,
  lowercase
};
```

Create a main file, `stringApp.js`:

```
// stringApp.js
const { uppercase, lowercase } =
require('./stringIndex');
console.log(uppercase("Hello Node!"));
console.log(lowercase("Hello Node!"));
```

Run:

```
node stringApp.js
```

Outcome:

```
HELLO NODE!
hello node!
```

Explanation:
You can combine multiple modules into one "index" file for easier imports. This approach helps keep your codebase organized when you have many related modules.

10 Multiple Choice Quiz Questions

1. **Which command initializes a default `package.json` file in your project folder?**
   A. `npm start`
   B. `npm init -y`
   C. `npm install`
   D. `node init`
   Correct Answer: B. `npm init -y`
   - ○ **Explanation**: The `-y` flag automatically answers all prompts with default values, creating a basic `package.json`.

2. **What is the purpose of the Node.js REPL?**
   A. To build production servers with zero configuration
   B. To interpret and run JavaScript commands interactively
   C. To bundle JavaScript files for the browser
   D. To install Node.js on your system
   Correct Answer: B. To interpret and run JavaScript commands interactively
   - ○ **Explanation**: The REPL (Read-Eval-Print Loop) lets you type JavaScript code line by line and see the results immediately.

3. **Which built-in Node.js method or property is used to read command-line arguments in your script?**
   A. `console.argv`
   B. `process.argv`
   C. `path.argv`
   D. `fs.argv`
   Correct Answer: B. `process.argv`
   - ○ **Explanation**: `process.argv` is an array containing the Node.js executable path, the script path, and any additional command-line arguments.

4. **When you want to export multiple functions from a single module using CommonJS, you typically use:**
   A. `export default`
   B. `require.all`
   C. `module.exports = { ... }`
   D. `import *`
   Correct Answer: C. `module.exports = { ... }`
   - **Explanation**: In CommonJS, you gather all the exports in an object assigned to `module.exports`. ES modules use `export` and `export default`.

What does the following script do?

```
#!/usr/bin/env node
console.log("Hello CLI");
```

5. A. Creates a global variable named `env`
   B. Tells the script to run under Node.js when executed directly from the CLI
   C. Opens the Node REPL
   D. Installs Node.js globally
   Correct Answer: B. Tells the script to run under Node.js when executed directly from the CLI
   - **Explanation**: The "shebang" line (`#!/usr/bin/env node`) allows the script to be run as an executable (e.g., `./script.js`), using the Node.js interpreter.

6. If you want to import a function named **divide** from an ES module file **math.mjs** in your **main.mjs**, which syntax do you use?

A. `const divide = require('math.mjs')`
B. `module.exports = { divide } from 'math.mjs'`
C. `import { divide } from './math.mjs'`
D. `export divide from 'math.mjs'`

Correct Answer: C. import { divide } from './math.mjs'

   o **Explanation**: With ES modules, you selectively import named exports using the curly brace syntax, referencing the path to the file.

7. **Which Node.js core module provides information about the current operating system?**

A. `os`
B. `path`
C. `http`
D. `crypto`

Correct Answer: A. os

   o **Explanation**: The `os` module offers methods to get details about the operating system (platform, CPU architecture, free memory, home directory, etc.).

8. **How do you exit the Node.js REPL?**

A. `.done`
B. `.exit` or `Ctrl + C` twice
C. `npm exit`
D. `process.exit()` is the only way

Correct Answer: B. .exit or Ctrl + C twice

   o **Explanation**: Node's REPL can be exited with the `.exit` command or by pressing `Ctrl + C` twice in succession.

9. **What is the primary difference between installing a package locally vs. globally with npm?**
   A. Globally installed packages cannot be used in your code
   B. Locally installed packages cannot be used in your code
   C. Global installs are available on the system PATH, while local installs stay in the project's `node_modules`
   D. There is no difference
   Correct Answer: C. Global installs are available on the system PATH, while local installs stay in the project's `node_modules`
   - ○ **Explanation**: A global install is typically used for CLI tools. Local installs remain project-specific under the `node_modules` folder.
10. **Which file typically defines your project's metadata, scripts, and dependencies in a Node.js project?**
   A. `index.js`
   B. `main.js`
   C. `package.json`
   D. `config.json`
   Correct Answer: C. `package.json`
   - ○ **Explanation**: The `package.json` file is the standard place to define a project's name, version, scripts, and dependencies.

Summary

In this section, you've:

- Learned how to install Node.js and optionally manage multiple versions.
- Explored the **Node REPL**, which is useful for quick one-off tests.
- Practiced **CommonJS** and **ES Modules** to structure your code.

- Mastered **npm** commands to manage your dependencies and create scripts for common tasks.
- Gained practical experience through 10 hands-on exercises and validated your knowledge with 10 quiz questions.

By applying these skills, you're well on your way to building robust Node.js applications. Next, we'll dive deeper into asynchronous programming, a core concept that powers Node's ability to handle many simultaneous operations efficiently.

Chapter 2. Setting Up Node.js

In this section, you'll learn how to install Node.js, verify your installation, initialize a basic Node.js project, and manage packages with **npm** (Node Package Manager). By the end, you'll be able to create a simple project structure and install external packages confidently.

1. Installing Node.js

1.1. Downloading from the Official Node.js Website

1. **Visit** https://nodejs.org and choose the version that suits your needs:
   - **LTS (Long-Term Support)** for stability.
   - **Current** for newer features.
2. **Run the installer**, following the on-screen instructions. This typically installs both **Node.js** and **npm**.

1.2. Verifying the Installation

Once installation is complete, open your terminal or command prompt and run:

```
node -v
npm -v
```

- **node -v** shows the Node.js version.
- **npm -v** shows the npm version.

If both commands return a version number, your installation was successful.

2. Setting Up a Basic Project

Node.js projects are typically organized around a `package.json` file, which holds information about the project and its dependencies.

2.1. Using npm init

Create a new folder for your project:

```
mkdir my-project
cd my-project
```
Initialize the project:

```
npm init -y
```

- The `-y` flag automatically answers all prompts with default values. If you want more customization, simply run `npm init` (without `-y`) and follow the interactive prompts.

2.2. Explanation of the package.json File

`package.json` is a critical file in Node.js projects. It typically includes:

- **Name**: The name of your project/package.
- **Version**: The current version of your project.

- **Description**: A short description of what your project does.
- **Scripts**: Custom command-line shortcuts (e.g., `npm run start`).
- **Dependencies**: Lists third-party packages that your project needs to function.
- **DevDependencies**: Lists packages used for development/testing, but not needed in production.

A simple `package.json` might look like:

```json
{
  "name": "my-project",
  "version": "1.0.0",
  "scripts": {
    "start": "node app.js"
  },
  "dependencies": {},
  "devDependencies": {}
}
```

3. Installing Packages

3.1. Introduction to npm (Node Package Manager)

npm is the default package manager for Node.js. It allows you to:

1. **Install packages** from the npm registry.
2. **Manage dependencies** (and their versions) within your project.
3. **Share your own packages** with others.

3.2. Example: Installing a Simple Package (e.g., nodemon)

`nodemon` is a popular development tool that automatically restarts your Node.js application when file changes are detected.

Install nodemon as a development dependency:

```
npm install --save-dev nodemon
```
Add a script in your `package.json`:

```
{
  "scripts": {
    "dev": "nodemon app.js"
  }
}
```
Start your app in dev mode:

```
npm run dev
```

- o Now, every time you change `app.js`, **nodemon** restarts the server automatically.

10 Coding Exercises

Below are ten hands-on exercises designed to reinforce your understanding of installing Node.js, initializing a project, and managing packages. Each exercise includes:

- **Learning Objective**: What you aim to learn or practice.
- **Outcome**: What you'll achieve or observe.
- **Full Code & Explanation** where applicable.

Exercise 1: Confirming Node and npm Versions

Learning Objective: Validate that Node.js and npm are installed and accessible on your system.

1. **Open** your terminal or command prompt.

Run:

```
node -v
npm -v
```

2. **Outcome**:
   - You'll see version numbers for both Node.js and npm.
   - If you get an error, revisit the installation steps.

Explanation:
This exercise ensures that your system recognizes the commands node and npm. Seeing version numbers confirms a successful installation.

Exercise 2: Creating a Basic package.json

Learning Objective: Familiarize yourself with the npm init command and the structure of package.json.

1. **Create** a folder named basic-package.

Navigate to that folder and run:

```
npm init
```

2. **Answer** the interactive prompts.
3. **Outcome**:
   - A package.json file is generated in basic-package.

- You'll see a name, version, description, and so on, as you specified.

Explanation:
This teaches you how to interact with npm init for a more customized setup, ensuring you understand the fields in package.json.

Exercise 3: Hello World App with npm Script

Learning Objective: Understand how npm scripts are defined and used to run simple Node.js programs.

Create a file called app.js in your project folder:

```
// app.js
console.log("Hello World from Node.js!");
```

Add a script to package.json:

```
{
  "scripts": {
    "start": "node app.js"
  }
}
```

Run:

```
npm run start
```

1. **Outcome**:
   - Terminal displays: Hello World from Node.js!

Explanation:
This shows how to link a simple Node.js program to an npm script, so you can start your app with a single command.

Exercise 4: Installing and Using a Third-Party Package

Learning Objective: Learn how to install packages and use them in your code.

Install the `color` package (a small utility for color formatting strings in the console):

```
npm install color
```

Create `colorExample.js`:

```
// colorExample.js
const Color = require("color");
const favoriteColor = Color("rgb(127, 255, 212)");
console.log("Hex value:", favoriteColor.hex());
console.log("Luminosity:", favoriteColor.luminosity());
```

Run:

```
node colorExample.js
```

1. **Outcome**:
   o Logs the hex value and luminosity of the specified color.

Explanation:
This demonstrates how to download a package from npm and use it within your Node.js script.

Exercise 5: Local vs. Global Installation

Learning Objective: Understand the difference between locally installing a package vs. installing it globally.

Globally install a small Node.js CLI tool (e.g., `serve` for serving local files):

```
npm install -g serve
```

1. **Navigate** to any directory with static files (HTML/CSS/JS).

Run:

```
serve
```

2. **Outcome**:
   - A simple HTTP server starts, serving the files on localhost at the displayed port.

Explanation:
Global packages are accessible anywhere from the command line (like `serve`). In contrast, **local** packages stay in `node_modules` inside your project folder.

Exercise 6: Dev Dependencies vs. Dependencies

Learning Objective: Learn how to separate packages needed for running vs. development/testing.

Install `nodemon` as a dev dependency:

```
npm install --save-dev nodemon
```

Update `package.json` scripts:

```
{
  "scripts": {
    "dev": "nodemon app.js"
  }
}
```

Run your dev script:

```
npm run dev
```

1. **Outcome**:
    - You see your `app.js` output in the console, and if you modify `app.js`, the process restarts automatically.

Explanation:
Installing a package with `--save-dev` places it in `devDependencies`, signaling it's only needed in development (e.g., debugging or testing tools).

Exercise 7: Exploring package-lock.json

Learning Objective: Understand how npm locks specific versions of dependencies for consistency.

Create a new project and install any package (e.g., `axios`):

```
npm init -y
npm install axios
```

1. **Observe** that a file named `package-lock.json` is created.
2. **Open** `package-lock.json` and look at the version details.

Outcome:
You'll see exact version references for `axios` and its dependencies, ensuring consistent installs across different environments.

Explanation:
`package-lock.json` is automatically generated. It locks down versions, so everyone who installs your project's dependencies gets the same version tree.

Exercise 8: Script to Output Environment Details

Learning Objective: Use Node.js scripts to gather and print environment info.

Create a file called `envInfo.js`:

```
// envInfo.js
console.log("Process ID:", process.pid);
console.log("Current Working Directory:",
process.cwd());
console.log("Node Version:",
process.version);
console.log("Platform:", process.platform);
```

Run:

```
node envInfo.js
```

1. **Outcome:**
   o Displays your process ID, working directory, Node.js version, and OS platform in the console.

Explanation:
By harnessing the global `process` object, you can gather valuable runtime information. This is often useful for debugging or logging.

Exercise 9: Creating a Custom Utility with npm init

Learning Objective: Practice packaging a small, reusable Node.js utility.

1. **Make** a new folder, say `string-tool`.

Initialize a new npm project:

```
npm init -y
```

Create `index.js`:

```
// index.js
function reverseString(str) {
  return str.split("").reverse().join("");
}
// Export this function so others can use it
module.exports = { reverseString };
```

2. **Outcome**:
   o You have a basic Node.js utility that can be published or shared.
   o Anyone installing your tool locally could `require` your reverseString function.

Explanation:
This outlines how easy it is to create your own package, define it in `package.json`, and export something. You could even publish it to npm if you wish!

Exercise 10: npm Scripts – Running Multiple Commands

Learning Objective: Learn how to define multiple tasks in npm scripts.

In your **package.json**, add:

```
{
  "scripts": {
    "say-hello": "echo Hello World!",
    "start-app": "node app.js",
    "all": "npm run say-hello && npm run
start-app"
  }
}
```

Create an app.js file that logs:

```
// app.js
console.log("App has started.");
```

Run:

```
npm run all
```

1. **Outcome**:
   ○ First, prints Hello World!
   ○ Then, runs node app.js and prints App has started.

Explanation:
You can chain scripts using && (run second command only if the first succeeds) or ; (run second command unconditionally). This is handy for bundling common tasks.

10 Multiple Choice Quiz Questions

Below are ten quiz questions to test your knowledge of Node.js installation, project setup, and npm usage. Detailed answers are provided for each.

1. **Which command do you use to create a new Node.js project with a package.json file?**
   A. `node init project`
   B. `npm init`
   C. `npm run create`
   D. `node create package.json`
   Correct Answer: B. npm init
   Explanation:
   - `npm init` starts the interactive process (or `npm init -y` uses defaults) to generate `package.json`.
2. **Where can you download the official installers for Node.js?**
   A. From any unofficial mirror site
   B. Through the npm registry
   C. From <u>nodejs.org</u>
   D. There is no official installer
   Correct Answer: C. From <u>nodejs.org</u>
   Explanation:
   - The Node.js website provides the official installers for different operating systems.
3. **Which file in a Node.js project typically contains the project's metadata and dependency information?**
   A. `index.js`
   B. `package.json`
   C. `package-lock.json`
   D. `node_modules/package.json`
   Correct Answer: B. package.json
   Explanation:
   - `package.json` includes the project's name, version, scripts, and dependencies.

4. **What is the purpose of `package-lock.json`?**
   A. It locks the Node.js version you can use
   B. It locks and records exact dependency versions
   C. It prevents other people from installing your dependencies
   D. It's a backup copy of `package.json`
   Correct Answer: B. It locks and records exact dependency versions
   Explanation:
   - `package-lock.json` ensures consistent, reproducible installations of dependencies.
5. **If you use `npm install --save-dev jest`, how is the dependency classified?**
   A. A global dependency
   B. A local runtime dependency
   C. A development (dev) dependency
   D. A peer dependency
   Correct Answer: C. A development (dev) dependency
   Explanation:
   - `--save-dev` adds packages to the `devDependencies` section of `package.json`.
6. **Which command verifies your Node.js version on the command line?**
   A. `npm -v`
   B. `node --check`
   C. `node -v`
   D. `npm --node-version`
   Correct Answer: C. `node -v`
   Explanation:
   - `node -v` prints the installed Node.js version. `npm -v` prints the installed npm version.

What does the following npm script do?

```
{
  "scripts": {
    "start": "node index.js"
```

```
    }
}
```

7. A. Automatically creates an `index.js` file
   B. Runs `index.js` when you type `npm start` in your terminal
   C. Installs `index.js` as a global module
   D. Creates a global alias for `node index.js`
   Correct Answer: B. Runs `index.js` when you type npm start in your terminal
   Explanation:
   - An npm script named `start` is triggered by `npm start`.

8. **Which option correctly installs a package globally?**
   A. `npm install mypackage`
   B. `npm install mypackage --global`
   C. `npm global mypackage`
   D. `npm global-install mypackage`
   Correct Answer: B. npm install mypackage --global (or -g)
   Explanation:
   - Using `--global` (or `-g`) is the standard way to install packages system-wide.

9. **In `package.json`, which section holds commands you can run with `npm run <command>`?**
   A. `"dependencies"`
   B. `"engines"`
   C. `"scripts"`
   D. `"main"`
   Correct Answer: C. "scripts"
   Explanation:
   - You define custom command-line tasks under the `"scripts"` object in `package.json`.

10. **After installing Node.js, how can you confirm that npm was also installed successfully?**
    A. By typing `node install npm`
    B. By running `npm -v` in the terminal
    C. By checking the local `node_modules` folder
    D. By installing a package without errors
    Correct Answer: B. By running `npm -v` in the terminal
    Explanation:
    - npm is bundled with Node.js, and `npm -v` quickly verifies the installed version.

Wrap-Up

You've now learned:

- **How to install Node.js** from the official website, verifying everything using `node -v` and `npm -v`.
- **How to set up a basic Node.js project** using `npm init`, including how to generate and understand `package.json`.
- **How to install packages** globally or locally, plus how dev dependencies differ from regular dependencies.
- **How to create and run npm scripts** to streamline your development workflow.

These foundational skills form the backbone of every Node.js project. By completing the coding exercises and quiz questions, you should feel comfortable setting up Node.js on your machine, initializing a new project, and managing its dependencies with npm. You're now ready to move on to more advanced Node.js topics, from asynchronous programming to building full-scale applications!

Chapter 3. Writing Your First Node.js Program

Building on what you've learned about installing Node.js and creating a basic project, this section focuses on writing and running your very first Node.js program—commonly the "Hello World" script—and understanding the Node.js Read-Eval-Print Loop (REPL). We'll explore how `console.log` works in Node.js, how to use the REPL to test snippets of code, and basic commands to help you become comfortable with an interactive Node.js environment.

1. "Hello World" Example

1.1. Writing a Simple Node.js Script

A classic first step in any programming language is to print "Hello World" to the console.

1. **Create** a file named `hello.js`.

Add the following code:

```
// hello.js
console.log("Hello World from Node.js!");
```
Run your script in the terminal:

```
node hello.js
```
Result:
You should see:

```
Hello World from Node.js!
```

2. displayed in your terminal.

1.2. How console.log Works

- `console.log()` prints its arguments to the standard output (usually the terminal).
- It automatically appends a newline at the end of each message.

This function is handy for simple debugging, logging intermediate values in your code, or quickly outputting results.

2. Understanding the Node.js REPL (Read-Eval-Print Loop)

The **Node.js REPL** allows you to run JavaScript code interactively, line by line, without creating a file.

Open your terminal and type:

```
node
```
You'll enter the REPL environment. You can now type any JavaScript expression:

```
> console.log("Hello from the REPL!");
Hello from the REPL!
```

1. **Press Enter** to see the evaluation immediately.
2. **Exit** the REPL by typing `.exit` or pressing `Ctrl + C` twice.

2.1. Basic Commands in the REPL

- `.help`: Lists special commands available in the REPL.
- `.exit`: Exits the REPL.
- `Ctrl + C` (twice): Another way to exit the REPL.
- **Up/Down Arrow Keys**: Cycle through your REPL command history.

Using the REPL is an excellent way to test small code snippets and explore JavaScript without writing a full script.

10 Coding Exercises

Below are ten coding exercises designed to help you practice writing Node.js programs and using the REPL. Each exercise includes:

1. **Learning Objective**: What you'll practice.
2. **Outcome**: What you'll see or learn.
3. **Full Code & Explanation**.

Exercise 1: Your First "Hello World" Script

Learning Objective

- Understand how to create and run a Node.js file with `console.log`.

Steps & Code

1. Create a file named `helloWorld.js`.

Write the following code:

```
// helloWorld.js
console.log("Hello World!");
```
Run the script:

```
node helloWorld.js
```

Outcome

- You will see `Hello World!` in your terminal.

Explanation

This establishes the basic workflow of Node.js: create a `.js` file, add JavaScript code, and run it with `node`.

Exercise 2: Using Variables and console.log

Learning Objective

- Practice declaring variables and printing them to the console.

Steps & Code

1. Create a file named `variables.js`.

Add the following:

```
// variables.js
let greeting = "Hello from a variable!";
let number = 42;
console.log(greeting);
console.log("The number is:", number);
```

Run the script:

```
node variables.js
```

Outcome

Outputs:

```
Hello from a variable!
The number is: 42
```

Explanation

You learn how `console.log` can display strings and numbers, showing them inline with helpful text.

Exercise 3: Basic Math in the REPL

Learning Objective

- Practice arithmetic directly in the REPL.

Steps

1. Open the Node REPL by typing `node` in your terminal.

Type:

```
> 5 + 7
12
> 9 * 3
27
> Math.pow(2, 5)
32
```

2. Press **Enter** after each command.

Outcome

- The REPL immediately prints the results of your arithmetic operations.

Explanation
The REPL can evaluate any JavaScript expression. You can quickly test calculations or functions without a separate script file.

Exercise 4: String Manipulation in the REPL

Learning Objective

- Explore string methods interactively.

Steps

1. Run node to open the REPL.

Type:

```
> let text = "Hello Node REPL";
> text.toUpperCase()
```

2. See how the REPL displays the result.

Outcome

- You discover how Node immediately evaluates JavaScript string methods, like .toUpperCase().

Explanation
This helps you experiment with JavaScript's standard library methods quickly.

Exercise 5: Creating a Multi-Line String

Learning Objective

- Use template literals to handle multi-line text in a single console.log statement.

Steps & Code

1. Create a file named multiLine.js.

Write:

```
// multiLine.js
const message = `
Hello,
This is a multi-line
string in Node.js!
`;
console.log(message);
```

Run:

```
node multiLine.js
```

Outcome

- Prints the multi-line text with line breaks as written.

Explanation
Template literals (using backticks ``) allow you to insert new lines without cumbersome string concatenation or escape characters.

Exercise 6: Simple Function in a Node.js File

Learning Objective

- Declare and use a function in your Node.js script, then log the output.

Steps & Code

Create `functionExample.js`:

```
// functionExample.js
function greet(name) {
  return `Hello, ${name}!`;
}
console.log(greet("Alice"));
console.log(greet("Bob"));
```
Run the file:

```
node functionExample.js
```

Outcome

```
Hello, Alice!
```

```
Hello, Bob!
```

Explanation

You're practicing how to define a function and use `console.log` to display its return values.

Exercise 7: Basic Input in the REPL

Learning Objective

- Use the built-in `readline` module in the REPL to see how you might handle user input (for demonstration only).

Steps

1. Open the REPL.

Require the `readline` module and create an interface:

```
> const readline =
require('readline').createInterface({
... input: process.stdin,
... output: process.stdout
... });
```

Ask for user input:

```
> readline.question("What's your name? ",
(name) => {
... console.log("Hello, " + name);
... readline.close();
... });
```

2. Type your name and press Enter.

Outcome

- The REPL prints a greeting with your input name.

54

Explanation

While typically you'd handle user input in a file, this example shows that the REPL can do more than just run immediate expressions; it can also handle asynchronous operations.

Exercise 8: Exploring Variables in the REPL

Learning Objective

- Experiment with variable scope and updates within the REPL.

Steps

1. Open the REPL with node.

Type:

```
> let count = 0;
> count++;
1
> count++;
2
> count
2
```

2. **Observe** how the value of count changes.

Outcome

- You see the variable persist in the REPL session until you exit, allowing repeated updates and queries.

Explanation

The REPL maintains a running context, which is helpful for testing code logic step by step.

Exercise 9: Checking Types with typeof in the REPL

Learning Objective

- Understand how to quickly verify the type of values.

Steps

In the REPL, type:

```
> typeof 42
> typeof "Hello"
> typeof true
> typeof undefined
> typeof {name: "Alice"}
```

1. Observe the output each time.

Outcome

- The REPL will print `'number'`, `'string'`, `'boolean'`, `'undefined'`, and `'object'` respectively.

Explanation

`typeof` is a quick way to check data types in JavaScript, and the REPL's immediacy helps you see the results right away.

Exercise 10: Using console.log with Multiple Arguments

Learning Objective

- Understand that `console.log` can handle multiple parameters, not just a single string.

Steps & Code

Create `multiArgs.js`:

```
// multiArgs.js
const name = "Charlie";
const age = 25;
console.log("Name:", name, "| Age:", age);
```

Run:

```
node multiArgs.js
```

Outcome

Outputs:

```
Name: Charlie | Age: 25
```

Explanation

Passing multiple arguments to `console.log` separates them by spaces (or the default delimiter). This is useful for logging multiple pieces of data in a single statement.

10 Multiple Choice Quiz Questions

Here are ten questions to test your understanding of writing your first Node.js program, using `console.log`, and exploring the REPL. Each answer includes a detailed explanation.

1. **Which command is used to run a JavaScript file in Node.js?**
   A. `npm start <filename.js>`
   B. `node <filename.js>`
   C. `node run <filename.js>`
   D. `npm <filename.js>`
   Correct Answer: B. `node <filename.js>`
   Explanation:
   - The basic way to execute a Node.js script is by using the `node` command followed by the script's file name.

2. **Which function in Node.js prints messages to the console?**

A. `window.alert`

B. `console.write`

C. `console.log`

D. `stdout.log`

Correct Answer: C. `console.log`

Explanation:

  - ○ In Node.js (and modern browsers), `console.log` is commonly used to output text or variable values to the console.

3. **When you type node in your terminal and press Enter, what environment are you starting?**

A. The Node.js package manager

B. A new Node.js project with `package.json`

C. The Node.js REPL (Read-Eval-Print Loop)

D. A Node.js debugger session

Correct Answer: C. The Node.js REPL (Read-Eval-Print Loop)

Explanation:

  - ○ `node` by itself launches an interactive environment for running JavaScript commands line by line.

4. **How do you exit the Node.js REPL?**

A. Type `Ctrl + D`

B. Type `.exit` or press `Ctrl + C` twice

C. Type `escape()` in the REPL

D. It cannot be exited once started

Correct Answer: B. Type `.exit` or press `Ctrl + C` twice

Explanation:

  - ○ `.exit` is a special REPL command. Pressing `Ctrl + C` two times is an alternative method.

5. Which statement about `console.log("Hello World");` in Node.js is true?
   A. It sends an alert message to the user's screen
   B. It writes the text "Hello World" to a file named `log.txt`
   C. It outputs "Hello World" to the terminal's standard output
   D. It only works in a browser environment
   Correct Answer: C. It outputs "Hello World" to the terminal's standard output
   Explanation:
   - `console.log` prints to the standard output where Node.js is running, usually a terminal or console environment.
6. **Which best describes the purpose of the REPL in Node.js?**
   A. A built-in testing framework for Node.js apps
   B. A browser simulator for front-end code
   C. An interactive shell to test JavaScript expressions without writing a file
   D. A library loader for external Node packages
   Correct Answer: C. An interactive shell to test JavaScript expressions without writing a file
   Explanation:
   - The REPL reads your input, evaluates it, prints the result, and loops for more input, providing immediate feedback.

7. **If you type `let x = 10; x` in the Node.js REPL, what will happen?**
   A. Nothing will happen because `let` is not allowed in the REPL
   B. It will assign `10` to `x` and print `10` as the final expression result
   C. It will terminate the REPL session
   D. It will throw a syntax error
   Correct Answer: B. It will assign `10` to `x` and print `10` as the final expression result
   Explanation:
   - The REPL prints the result of the last expression. Declaring `x = 10;` then typing `x` outputs the current value of `x`.

8. **Which of the following is not a typical use of `console.log`?**
   A. Logging debugging information
   B. Printing results in a Node.js script
   C. Writing data to a remote database
   D. Displaying messages in the REPL
   Correct Answer: C. Writing data to a remote database
   Explanation:
   - `console.log` only prints to the console. It does not handle network or database operations.

9. **What is the correct way to run a JavaScript expression in the Node.js REPL?**
   A. Start the REPL with `npm start`, then type the expression
   B. Type `node run` followed by the expression
   C. Type `node`, press Enter, then type your expression and press Enter again
   D. You cannot directly run expressions in the REPL without creating a file
   Correct Answer: C. Type `node`, press Enter, then type your expression and press Enter again
   Explanation:

- This is the workflow for using the REPL: `node` starts it, and you can then type your JavaScript expressions line by line.
10. **How does `console.log("Value:", 123, true)` appear in the console output by default?**
   A. `Value:, 123, true` (all comma separated)
   B. `Value: 123 true` (with spaces between arguments)
   C. `[ "Value:", 123, true ]` (array format)
   D. `undefined`
   Correct Answer: B. `Value: 123 true` (with spaces between arguments)
   Explanation:
   - By default, `console.log` inserts spaces between multiple arguments, so each argument is output in sequence with a space separating them.

Summary

In this section, you learned how to:

1. Write your first Node.js program, commonly known as the "Hello World" script.
2. Use `console.log` to display messages and values in the terminal.
3. Work with the Node.js REPL, an interactive environment perfect for quick tests and JavaScript experiments.
4. Utilize basic REPL commands and build confidence in running JavaScript code without needing separate files.

Completing these exercises and quiz questions helps solidify your foundation in Node.js. Now that you can write and run basic programs—and test snippets in the REPL—you're ready to explore asynchronous programming, build simple servers, and dive deeper into the Node.js ecosystem!

Chapter 4. Node.js Core Modules

Node.js comes with a set of **core modules** that you can use without any additional installation. These modules provide essential functionalities such as file manipulation, network operations, handling paths, and accessing operating system details. This section introduces what core modules are, highlights some commonly used modules, and walks you through practical examples of `fs`, `path`, `os`, and `http`.

1. Introduction to Core Modules

1.1. What Are Core Modules?

- **Definition**: Core modules are built-in libraries that ship with Node.js. They are written in C++ and JavaScript, providing low-level functionality directly accessible via `require('moduleName')` or (in newer code) `import moduleName from 'moduleName'` without needing to install anything from npm.
- **Purpose**: They handle foundational tasks (e.g., file operations, networking) so you can develop server-side applications without always relying on third-party packages.

1.2. Commonly Used Modules

1. **`fs` (File System)**: Read, write, and manipulate files.
2. **`path`**: Work with file and directory paths across different operating systems.

3. **os**: Retrieve OS-level information (e.g., CPU, memory).
4. **http**: Create HTTP servers and handle requests/responses.
5. **events**: Implement custom event-driven patterns.
6. **crypto**: Perform cryptographic operations, like hashing.
7. **util**: Provide utility functions for debugging, promisifying callbacks, etc.

2. Examples of Core Modules

In this section, we'll cover four popular core modules (`fs`, `path`, `os`, and `http`) with practical code samples. Each example uses the CommonJS syntax (`require()`), but you can also use ES modules (`import`) if your project is configured accordingly.

2.1. fs: Reading and Writing Files

Reading a File Asynchronously

```
const fs = require('fs');
fs.readFile('example.txt', 'utf8', (err,
data) => {
  if (err) {
    return console.error('Error reading
file:', err);
  }
  console.log('File contents:', data);
});
```

- **Explanation**:
    - `fs.readFile()` reads the file `example.txt` asynchronously.
    - If successful, the `data` is printed to the console; if not, the error is logged.

Writing to a File

```
const fs = require('fs');
const content = 'Some text to write into the
file.';
fs.writeFile('output.txt', content, (err) =>
{
  if (err) {
    return console.error('Error writing
file:', err);
  }
  console.log('File written successfully!');
});
```

- Explanation:
    - fs.writeFile() creates or overwrites
      output.txt with the text in content.
    - On success, you see a confirmation message.

2.2. path: Working with File Paths

Building a Path

```
const path = require('path');
const directory = 'user';
const filename = 'data.json';
const fullPath = path.join(__dirname,
directory, filename);
console.log('Full path:', fullPath);
```

- Explanation:
    - path.join() constructs a path string using
      the appropriate directory separators for the
      operating system.
    - __dirname is a Node.js global variable
      indicating the directory of the current file.

Extracting File Extensions

```
const path = require('path');
const filePath = '/home/project/index.html';
console.log('Extension:',
path.extname(filePath)); // Output: .html
```

- **Explanation**:
    - `path.extname(filePath)` returns the extension of the path, such as `.html` or `.js`.

2.3. os: System Information

Retrieving CPU Details

```
const os = require('os');
const cpus = os.cpus();
console.log('CPU Info:', cpus);
```

- **Explanation**:
    - `os.cpus()` returns an array of objects detailing each logical CPU core's information.

Memory Information

```
const os = require('os');
console.log('Total Memory:', os.totalmem());
console.log('Free Memory:', os.freemem());
```

- **Explanation**:
    - `os.totalmem()` returns the total system memory in bytes.
    - `os.freemem()` returns the free system memory, also in bytes.

2.4. http: Creating a Basic HTTP Server

Simple HTTP Server

```
const http = require('http');
const server = http.createServer((req, res)
=> {
  res.writeHead(200, { 'Content-Type':
'text/plain' });
  res.end('Hello from Node.js HTTP server!');
});
server.listen(3000, () => {
  console.log('Server is running on
http://localhost:3000');
});
```

- **Explanation**:
    - `http.createServer()` sets up a basic server, which listens for requests on port 3000.
    - `res.writeHead(200, ...)` sets the response status to 200 and specifies a `Content-Type`.
    - `res.end(...)` sends the response to the client.

10 Coding Exercises

Below are ten exercises designed to help you practice using Node.js core modules. Each exercise provides:

- **Learning Objective**
- **Outcome**
- **Full Code & Explanation**

Feel free to adapt file names and folder structure as needed.

Exercise 1: Reading a File with fs.readFile

Learning Objective: Practice asynchronous file reading using the `fs` module.

1. **Create** a file named `readFileExercise.js`.

Write the following code:

```
// readFileExercise.js
const fs = require('fs');
fs.readFile('sample.txt', 'utf8', (err, data)
=> {
  if (err) {
    return console.error('Could not read
file:', err);
  }
  console.log('Contents of sample.txt:',
data);
});
```

2. **Outcome**:
   - ○ Displays the content of `sample.txt` in the terminal if the file exists.

Explanation:

- This solidifies your understanding of how Node's asynchronous API works. If you run `node` `readFileExercise.js` and `sample.txt` doesn't exist, you'll see an error message.

Exercise 2: Writing a File with fs.writeFile

Learning Objective: Learn to create a new file or overwrite an existing file using the `fs` module.

Create `writeFileExercise.js`:

```
// writeFileExercise.js
const fs = require('fs');
```

```
const data = 'This is some text for the
file.';
fs.writeFile('myFile.txt', data, (err) => {
  if (err) {
    return console.error('Failed to write
file:', err);
  }
  console.log('File has been written!');
});
```

1. **Run** node writeFileExercise.js.
2. **Outcome**:
   - Creates or overwrites myFile.txt with the specified text.

Explanation:

- Writing files is common for logging, saving user data, or exporting reports.

Exercise 3: Appending to a File

Learning Objective: Practice adding content to an existing file without overwriting it.

Create appendFileExercise.js:

```
// appendFileExercise.js
const fs = require('fs');
const logEntry = `Logged at ${new
Date().toISOString()}\n`;
fs.appendFile('log.txt', logEntry, (err) => {
  if (err) {
    return console.error('Failed to append to
file:', err);
  }
```

```
console.log('Log entry added:',
logEntry.trim());
});
```

1. **Run** it multiple times to see multiple entries appended.
2. **Outcome**:
   - o   `log.txt` grows with each new line timestamp.

Explanation:

- Appending is useful for maintaining logs, incremental data, or versioned text.

Exercise 4: Using path to Build a Dynamic File Path

Learning Objective: Learn how to safely construct file paths for cross-platform compatibility.

Create pathExercise.js:

```
// pathExercise.js
const path = require('path');
// Suppose we have a logs folder and a file
name
const logDir = 'logs';
const logFile = 'app.log';
// This script is in the current directory
const fullPath = path.join(__dirname, logDir,
logFile);
console.log('Full log path:', fullPath);
```

1. **Run** node pathExercise.js.
2. **Outcome**:

- Prints a path like
  /Users/<user>/<project>/logs/app.lo
  g on Unix or C:\Users\<user>\... on
  Windows.

Explanation:

- This ensures your scripts work reliably across different operating systems without manually handling directory separators.

Exercise 5: Normalizing and Parsing Paths

Learning Objective: Understand path.normalize() and path.parse() for path manipulation.

Create pathParseExercise.js:

```
// pathParseExercise.js
const path = require('path');
const messyPath =
'/Users//someuser\\projects//demo/../app.js';
console.log('Normalized path:',
path.normalize(messyPath));
const parsed = path.parse(messyPath);
console.log('Parsed path object:', parsed);
```

1. **Run** node pathParseExercise.js.
2. **Outcome**:
   - path.normalize() cleans up redundant slashes and .. segments.
   - path.parse() returns an object with root, dir, base, ext, name.

Explanation:

70

- Normalizing paths can save you from file not found errors. Parsing helps you extract details like base name or extension.

Exercise 6: Checking OS Platform and CPU Architecture

Learning Objective: Use the os module to gather system-level info.

Create osExercise.js:

```
// osExercise.js
const os = require('os');
console.log('Operating System:',
os.platform());
console.log('CPU Architecture:', os.arch());
```

1. **Run** node osExercise.js.
2. **Outcome**:
   ○ Displays the OS (e.g., win32, darwin, linux) and architecture (x64, etc.).

Explanation:

- This is especially useful if your program has platform-specific or architecture-specific logic.

Exercise 7: Listing System Network Interfaces

Learning Objective: Explore os.networkInterfaces() to see available network interfaces.

Create netInfoExercise.js:

```
// netInfoExercise.js
```

```
const os = require('os');
const interfaces = os.networkInterfaces();
console.log('Network Interfaces:',
interfaces);
```

1. **Run** node netInfoExercise.js.
2. **Outcome**:
   o Prints an object containing data about each
     network interface (e.g., Wi-Fi, Ethernet).

Explanation:

- This can help you identify local IP addresses, MAC
  addresses, and more.

Exercise 8: Creating a Basic HTTP Server

Learning Objective: Start an HTTP server on a given port
and respond with plain text.

Create httpServerExercise.js:

```
// httpServerExercise.js
const http = require('http');
const server = http.createServer((req, res)
=> {
  res.writeHead(200, { 'Content-Type':
'text/plain' });
  res.end('Hello World from my first Node.js
server!');
});
server.listen(4000, () => {
  console.log('Server is running at
http://localhost:4000');
});
```

Run:

```
node httpServerExercise.js
```

1. **Outcome**:
   - Visit `http://localhost:4000` in your browser to see the message.

Explanation:

- Showcases how to use Node's built-in `http` module to handle incoming requests and send out responses.

Exercise 9: Returning JSON with http

Learning Objective: Send a JSON response using the `http` module.

Create `jsonServerExercise.js`:

```
// jsonServerExercise.js
const http = require('http');
const server = http.createServer((req, res)
=> {
  const responseObject = {
    status: 'success',
    data: {
      message: 'Here is some JSON data!'
    }
  };
  res.writeHead(200, { 'Content-Type':
'application/json' });
  res.end(JSON.stringify(responseObject));
});
server.listen(5000, () => {
```

```
    console.log('JSON server running at
http://localhost:5000');
});
```

1. **Outcome**:
   - o Go to http://localhost:5000, and you'll
      see JSON displayed in the browser.

Explanation:

- Useful for building RESTful APIs. You can send
  structured data, such as configuration or database
  results, to the client.

Exercise 10: File Server Using http and fs

Learning Objective: Combine the http and fs modules to
serve an HTML file.

Create fileServerExercise.js:

```
// fileServerExercise.js
const http = require('http');
const fs = require('fs');
const path = require('path');
const server = http.createServer((req, res)
=> {
  // Serve an index.html if user hits the
root URL
  if (req.url === '/') {
    const filePath = path.join(__dirname,
'index.html');
    fs.readFile(filePath, 'utf8', (err, data)
=> {
      if (err) {
```

```
        res.writeHead(500, { 'Content-Type':
'text/plain' });
        return res.end('Error loading
index.html');
      }
      res.writeHead(200, { 'Content-Type':
'text/html' });
      res.end(data);
    });
  } else {
    res.writeHead(404, { 'Content-Type':
'text/plain' });
    res.end('Not Found');
  }
});
server.listen(3001, () => {
  console.log('File server running at
http://localhost:3001');
});
```

Create an index.html file in the same folder:

```
<!-- index.html -->
<!DOCTYPE html>
<html>
<head>
  <title>Node.js File Server</title>
</head>
<body>
  <h1>Hello from a basic Node File
Server!</h1>
</body>
</html>
```

1. **Outcome**:
   o When you visit http://localhost:3001, the
     server will read and serve index.html.

Explanation:

- Demonstrates how to combine file operations (`fs`) with HTTP request handling to serve static content.

10 Multiple Choice Quiz Questions

1. **Which statement best describes Node.js core modules?**
   A. They are third-party libraries that must be installed via npm
   B. They come bundled with Node.js and can be required without installation
   C. They only work on Linux-based systems
   D. They are deprecated modules that no longer work
   Correct Answer: B. They come bundled with Node.js and can be required without installation
   Explanation:
   - Core modules are built into Node.js itself and don't need to be installed from npm.

2. **Which core module would you use to build a networked HTTP service?**
   A. `fs`
   B. `http`
   C. `crypto`
   D. `path`
   Correct Answer: B. `http`
   Explanation:
   - The `http` module enables creating an HTTP server and handling incoming requests and outgoing responses.

3. **What is the primary purpose of the fs module?**
   A. To create HTTP servers
   B. To manage file and directory operations
   C. To parse JSON data
   D. To execute shell commands
   Correct Answer: B. To manage file and directory operations
   Explanation:
   - The fs (File System) module deals with reading, writing, and manipulating files.

4. **Which function would you use to construct a normalized file path with the path module?**
   A. `path.readFile()`
   B. `path.fs()`
   C. `path.join()`
   D. `path.createServer()`
   Correct Answer: C. `path.join()`
   Explanation:
   - `path.join()` combines multiple path segments into a normalized path string.

5. **Which method in the os module returns information about each CPU core?**
   A. `os.arch()`
   B. `os.cpus()`
   C. `os.freemem()`
   D. `os.platform()`
   Correct Answer: B. `os.cpus()`
   Explanation:
   - `os.cpus()` returns an array of objects describing each logical CPU core on the system.

6. **If you want to serve static HTML files in Node.js without a framework like Express, which two modules are typically used together?**
   A. `fs` and `http`
   B. `path` and `events`
   C. `crypto` and `fs`
   D. `os` and `http`
   Correct Answer: A. `fs` and `http`
   Explanation:
   - `http` lets you create a server, while `fs` reads the HTML file from disk to serve to clients.

7. **Which HTTP status code indicates a successful response?**
   A. `404`
   B. `500`
   C. `200`
   D. `301`
   Correct Answer: C. `200`
   Explanation:
   - HTTP `200 OK` signals a successful request and response.

8. **Which `fs` method is used to add content to an existing file without overwriting it?**
   A. `fs.writeFile()`
   B. `fs.appendFile()`
   C. `fs.readFile()`
   D. `fs.copyFile()`
   Correct Answer: B. `fs.appendFile()`
   Explanation:
   - `appendFile()` appends data to a file; `writeFile()` overwrites or creates the file from scratch.

9. **Which method do you call to start listening for requests on an HTTP server created by `http.createServer()`?**
   A. `server.listen()`
   B. `server.run()`
   C. `server.bind()`
   D. `server.connect()`
   Correct Answer: A. `server.listen()`
   Explanation:
   - `server.listen()` specifies the port and optional hostname for the server to accept incoming requests.
10. **If you only want the file extension (`.txt`, `.js`, etc.) from a file path, which `path` method do you use?**
    A. `path.basename()`
    B. `path.extname()`
    C. `path.dirname()`
    D. `path.parse()`
    Correct Answer: B. `path.extname()`
    Explanation:
    - `path.extname(filename)` retrieves the extension portion of the filename, including the preceding dot.

Summary

- **Core Modules Overview**: Node.js core modules come prepackaged, saving you from installing extra libraries for essential features.
- **fs**: Manage file operations like reading, writing, and appending.
- **path**: Work with file and directory paths in a system-independent way.
- **os**: Gather information about the operating system, such as CPU details and memory usage.

- **http**: Build HTTP servers and handle requests/responses—key for web services and APIs.

Through the 10 coding exercises, you should now be more comfortable reading and writing files, handling path manipulations, extracting OS details, and serving HTTP responses. Mastering these core modules equips you with the tools to build more advanced and varied Node.js applications.

Chapter 5. Building a Simple HTTP Server

In this chapter, you'll learn how to create and run a simple HTTP server using Node.js. While we touched on the http module in the previous section, here we'll provide new and more detailed examples, as well as 10 practical coding exercises to reinforce your understanding of how a Node.js server works. By the end, you'll be comfortable starting a basic server, responding to HTTP requests, and verifying everything in your browser.

1. Creating a Basic Server

1.1 Using the http Module

The http module is a core Node.js module that allows you to create an HTTP server, handle incoming requests, and send responses back to the client.

Example: Basic HTTP Server (Port 3000)

```
// basicServer.js
const http = require('http');
// Create the server
```

```javascript
const server = http.createServer((req, res)
=> {
  // Set the response header: status code and
content type
  res.writeHead(200, { 'Content-Type':
'text/plain' });
  // Send the response body
  res.end('Hello from Node.js!');
});
// Start the server on port 3000
server.listen(3000, () => {
  console.log('Server is running at
http://localhost:3000');
});
```

Explanation:

1. We import the `http` module via `require('http')`.
2. `http.createServer((req, res) => {...})` creates a new server instance that listens for HTTP requests.
3. Within the callback, we define how to handle each incoming request using `req` (request) and `res` (response).
4. We then specify a `Content-Type` header of `"text/plain"` and finalize the response with `res.end(...)`.
5. Finally, `server.listen(3000, ...)` makes the server listen on port `3000`.

2. Running and Testing the Server

1. **Save** the file as `basicServer.js` (or any name you prefer).
2. **Open** a terminal in the same directory as the file.

Run:

```
node basicServer.js
```

3. **Visit** `http://localhost:3000` in your web browser.
4. **Observe** the message "Hello from Node.js!" displayed in your browser window.

Key Takeaways:

- Node.js servers run perpetually until you stop them (usually by pressing `Ctrl + C` in the terminal).
- You can choose any open port (e.g., 3000, 5000, 8080), but 3000 is a common default in tutorials.

10 Coding Exercises

Below are ten exercises designed to build your skill set in creating and working with Node.js HTTP servers. Each exercise has:

1. **Learning Objective**
2. **Detailed Code Example**
3. **Outcome** (what you'll observe when running it)
4. **Explanation**

Feel free to adapt ports, file names, or any other details to fit your development environment.

Exercise 1: A Server that Greets with Your Name

Learning Objective

- Introduce dynamic content in the HTTP response.

```
// serverName.js
```

```
const http = require('http');
const server = http.createServer((req, res)
=> {
  const name = 'Alice'; // Replace with your
own or retrieve from a variable
  res.writeHead(200, { 'Content-Type':
'text/plain' });
  res.end(`Hello, ${name}, from your Node.js
server!`);
});
server.listen(3001, () => {
  console.log('Name-based server running at
http://localhost:3001');
});
```

Outcome

- When you visit `http://localhost:3001`, you'll see "Hello, Alice, from your Node.js server!"

Explanation

- Hardcoding a variable is a simple step toward customizing responses. Later, you could make this more dynamic by reading from a config file, environment variable, or query parameter.

Exercise 2: Multiple Routes in a Single Server

Learning Objective

- Learn how to check `req.url` to serve different responses based on the route.

```
// multiRouteServer.js
const http = require('http');
```

```javascript
const server = http.createServer((req, res)
=> {
  if (req.url === '/') {
    res.writeHead(200, { 'Content-Type':
'text/plain' });
    res.end('Welcome to the Home Page!');
  } else if (req.url === '/about') {
    res.writeHead(200, { 'Content-Type':
'text/plain' });
    res.end('This is the About Page.');
  } else {
    res.writeHead(404, { 'Content-Type':
'text/plain' });
    res.end('Page Not Found.');
  }
});
server.listen(3002, () => {
  console.log('Multi-route server running at
http://localhost:3002');
});
```

Outcome

- Visiting http://localhost:3002 shows "Welcome to the Home Page!"
- Visiting http://localhost:3002/about shows "This is the About Page."
- Any other path shows a 404 error message.

Explanation

- req.url indicates the path requested by the client. By checking its value, you can serve different pages without external frameworks.

Exercise 3: Using Environment Variables for the Port

Learning Objective

- Understand how to use environment variables to configure your server's port, falling back to a default when none is provided.

```
// envPortServer.js
const http = require('http');
const PORT = process.env.PORT || 3003;
const server = http.createServer((req, res)
=> {
  res.writeHead(200, { 'Content-Type':
'text/plain' });
  res.end(`Server running on port ${PORT}`);
});
server.listen(PORT, () => {
  console.log(`Server is listening on port
${PORT}`);
});
```

Outcome

- If you run PORT=4000 node envPortServer.js in your terminal, it listens on 4000.
- If you run node envPortServer.js without specifying PORT, it defaults to 3003.

Explanation

- Environment variables are frequently used in production to avoid hardcoding server configurations.

Exercise 4: Returning JSON Data

Learning Objective

- Show how to return JSON for building a simple REST-like service.

```javascript
// jsonServer.js
const http = require('http');
const server = http.createServer((req, res)
=> {
  const data = {
    message: 'Hello JSON',
    timestamp: new Date().toISOString()
  };
  res.writeHead(200, { 'Content-Type':
'application/json' });
  res.end(JSON.stringify(data));
});
server.listen(3004, () => {
  console.log('JSON server running at
http://localhost:3004');
});
```

Outcome

Visiting `http://localhost:3004` returns a JSON object, e.g.:

```json
{
  "message": "Hello JSON",
  "timestamp": "2025-01-01T12:00:00.000Z"
}
```

Explanation

- Setting `Content-Type` to `application/json` signals to clients (browsers, APIs) that the response is valid JSON.

Exercise 5: Logging Requests

Learning Objective

- Learn to log incoming request details (`req.method` and `req.url`) for debugging or analytics.

```
// loggingServer.js
const http = require('http');
const server = http.createServer((req, res)
=> {
  console.log(`Received request:
${req.method} ${req.url}`);
  res.writeHead(200, { 'Content-Type':
'text/plain' });
  res.end('Request logged to console');
});
server.listen(3005, () => {
  console.log('Logging server running at
http://localhost:3005');
});
```

Outcome

- Each time you request a URL (e.g. `/`, `/test`), it logs something like `Received request: GET /test` in your terminal and responds with "Request logged to console."

Explanation

- `req.method` is usually `"GET"`, `"POST"`, `"PUT"`, etc. Logging helps you track requests in real-time.

Exercise 6: Handling Query Parameters Manually

Learning Objective

- Parse query parameters (without external libraries) from the URL.

```
// queryServer.js
const http = require('http');
const url = require('url');
const server = http.createServer((req, res)
=> {
  const parsedUrl = url.parse(req.url, true);
// 'true' parses query as an object
  const name = parsedUrl.query.name ||
'Stranger';
  res.writeHead(200, { 'Content-Type':
'text/plain' });
  res.end(`Hello, ${name}!`);
});
server.listen(3006, () => {
  console.log('Query server running at
http://localhost:3006');
});
```

Outcome

- Visiting http://localhost:3006/?name=Alice yields "Hello, Alice!"
- Visiting http://localhost:3006/ (with no query) yields "Hello, Stranger!"

Explanation

- Node's built-in url.parse can extract query parameters. In modern Node.js versions, you might also use new URL(req.url, baseURL).

Exercise 7: Serving Simple HTML

Learning Objective

- Send an HTML response to the browser instead of plain text or JSON.

```
// htmlServer.js
const http = require('http');
const server = http.createServer((req, res)
=> {
  const html = `
    <!DOCTYPE html>
    <html>
    <head><title>Node HTML</title></head>
    <body>
      <h1>Hello from an HTML Response!</h1>
      <p>This is a simple HTML page served by
Node.js.</p>
    </body>
    </html>
  `;
  res.writeHead(200, { 'Content-Type':
'text/html' });
  res.end(html);
});
server.listen(3007, () => {
  console.log('HTML server running at
http://localhost:3007');
});
```

Outcome

- At http://localhost:3007, you'll see a simple HTML page with a heading and paragraph text.

Explanation

- The `Content-Type` here is `text/html`, so browsers know to render the returned string as an HTML page.

Exercise 8: Handling Different Methods (GET vs. POST)

Learning Objective

- Demonstrate how to check `req.method` to respond differently to GET or POST requests.

```
// methodServer.js
const http = require('http');
const server = http.createServer((req, res)
=> {
  if (req.method === 'GET') {
    res.writeHead(200, { 'Content-Type':
'text/plain' });
    res.end('You made a GET request');
  } else if (req.method === 'POST') {
    res.writeHead(200, { 'Content-Type':
'text/plain' });
    res.end('You made a POST request');
  } else {
    res.writeHead(405, { 'Content-Type':
'text/plain' });
    res.end('Method not allowed');
  }
});
server.listen(3008, () => {
  console.log('Method server running at
http://localhost:3008');
});
```

Outcome

- A GET request to / returns "You made a GET request."
- A POST request (e.g., via a REST client or `curl -X POST http://localhost:3008`) returns "You made a POST request."
- Any other HTTP method (PUT, DELETE, etc.) returns "Method not allowed."

Explanation

- Checking `req.method` is essential for building RESTful APIs or handling form submissions.

Exercise 9: Custom Headers and Status Codes

Learning Objective

- Learn how to set your own HTTP status codes and custom headers in the response.

```
// customHeaderServer.js
const http = require('http');
const server = http.createServer((req, res)
=> {
  // For demonstration, send a 202 (Accepted)
status code
  res.writeHead(202, {
    'Content-Type': 'text/plain',
    'X-Custom-Header': 'LearningNode'
  });
  res.end('Custom status code and header
sent.');
});
server.listen(3009, () => {
  console.log('Custom header server at
http://localhost:3009');
});
```

Outcome

- Inspect the response in your browser's developer tools or via a tool like `curl -I http://localhost:3009`, and you'll see:
  - `HTTP/1.1 202 Accepted`
  - `X-Custom-Header: LearningNode`

Explanation

- By using `res.writeHead(statusCode, headersObject)`, you control the status code and any headers you want to set.

Exercise 10: Graceful Shutdown on SIGINT

Learning Objective

- Show how to properly close an HTTP server when receiving an interrupt signal (Ctrl + C).

```
// gracefulShutdown.js
const http = require('http');
const server = http.createServer((req, res)
=> {
  res.end('Graceful shutdown demo server');
});
server.listen(3010, () => {
  console.log('Graceful server at
http://localhost:3010');
});
process.on('SIGINT', () => {
  console.log('\nReceived SIGINT. Shutting
down...');
  server.close(() => {
    console.log('HTTP server closed.
Goodbye!');
```

```
    process.exit(0); // Exit the process
  });
});
```

Outcome

- When you press `Ctrl + C`, it logs a shutdown message, closes the server, and then ends the process.

Explanation

- Handling signals ensures your server releases resources (like open sockets) gracefully rather than abruptly terminating.

10 Multiple Choice Quiz Questions

Test your knowledge of building a basic Node.js HTTP server. Each question is followed by a detailed explanation.

1. **Which core Node.js module is used for creating HTTP servers?**
   A. `fs`
   B. `path`
   C. `http`
   D. `net`
   Correct Answer: C. `http`
   Explanation:
   - The `http` module provides the functionality to create and manage HTTP servers, handle requests, and send responses.

2. **Which method starts your Node.js server listening on a specific port?**

A. `server.run()`

B. `server.start()`

C. `server.init()`

D. `server.listen()`

Correct Answer: D. `server.listen()`

Explanation:
- o After creating a server instance with `http.createServer()`, you call `server.listen(PORT, callback)` to start it listening on the specified port.

3. **What is the default status code returned if you do not explicitly set one in your response?**

A. `200 OK`

B. `404 Not Found`

C. `500 Internal Server Error`

D. `301 Moved Permanently`

Correct Answer: A. `200 OK`

Explanation:
- o If you don't set a status code via `res.writeHead(...)` or `res.statusCode`, Node.js defaults to `200 OK`.

4. **Which of the following is not a property on the `req` (request) object in the HTTP server callback?**

A. `req.method`

B. `req.url`

C. `req.statusCode`

D. `req.headers`

Correct Answer: C. `req.statusCode`

Explanation:
- o The `req` object represents the incoming request, which includes `method`, `url`, and `headers`. `statusCode` is part of the response object (`res`), not the request.

5. **Why might you set a custom header such as X-Custom-Header?**
A. To output HTML instead of JSON
B. To override the request method
C. To pass additional, custom metadata to the client
D. To reduce server load
Correct Answer: C. To pass additional, custom metadata to the client
Explanation:
  - Custom headers can convey extra information about the response (e.g., version info, environment data) not covered by standard headers.

6. **Which statement best describes the `Content-Type` header in an HTTP response?**
A. It specifies the accepted request methods (GET, POST, PUT, etc.)
B. It indicates the type of data in the response (e.g., `text/html`, `application/json`)
C. It is only relevant for error messages
D. It is set automatically without developer control
Correct Answer: B. It indicates the type of data in the response (e.g., `text/html`, `application/json`)
Explanation:
  - Setting the `Content-Type` tells the client how to interpret the response body. For instance, `text/html` instructs browsers to parse the response as HTML.

7. **How would you typically stop a running Node.js server launched via `node server.js` in the terminal?**
A. Call `server.stop()` in your code
B. Press `Ctrl + C` in the terminal
C. There is no way to stop it once started
D. By removing the `http` module
Correct Answer: B. Press `Ctrl + C` in the terminal
Explanation:

- Pressing `Ctrl + C` sends the `SIGINT` signal, which terminates the Node.js process unless you handle it gracefully in your code.

8. **If you want to build different responses for paths like / and /about, how would you differentiate them in your server callback?**
   A. By checking `req.statusCode`
   B. By using `req.url` in conditional statements
   C. By setting `res.url` in the callback
   D. By specifying different ports for each path
   Correct Answer: B. By using `req.url` in conditional statements
   Explanation:
   - You can compare `req.url` to specific path strings (e.g., /, /about) to generate the appropriate response.

9. **Which of the following correctly sets a JSON response with status code 200?**

```
A. res.writeHead('application/json');
res.end(JSON.stringify({ msg: 'OK' }));
B. res.writeHead(200, { 'Content-Type':
'text/json' }); res.end({ msg: 'OK' });
C. res.writeHead(200, { 'Content-Type':
'application/json' });
res.end(JSON.stringify({ msg: 'OK' }));
D. res.statusCode = 200;   res.end("{
msg: 'OK' }");
```
   Correct Answer: C
   Explanation:
   - You need to pass the numeric status code (e.g., 200) and a valid MIME type for JSON (`application/json`). Also, the response body must be a JSON string, which `JSON.stringify` handles.

10. **Which method on the `http` server is used to respond and finalize the request?**

    A. `res.complete()`

    B. `res.end()`

    C. `res.writeHead()`

    D. `res.close()`

    Correct Answer: B. **`res.end()`**

    Explanation:
    - `res.end()` indicates that you have finished sending data for this response. Once called, the connection is considered complete for that request.

Conclusion

In this section, you built a simple HTTP server in Node.js using the `http` module, learned to respond to basic requests, and tested your server by accessing `http://localhost:3000` (or other ports). The exercises showcased practical tasks like logging requests, serving HTML or JSON, handling different methods, and implementing graceful shutdown.

This foundation is crucial for creating any web-based Node.js application. With these skills, you can now expand into more complex routing, handle file uploads, integrate databases, or move on to frameworks like Express.js. Keep experimenting with the exercises to deepen your understanding, and soon you'll be confident handling all kinds of HTTP-driven tasks in Node.js!

Chapter 6. Working with the File System

Node.js provides powerful built-in tools for interacting with the file system through the `fs` module. In this chapter, we'll explore how to read and write files asynchronously, and then apply these concepts to a practical example — logging incoming HTTP requests to a file. By the end, you'll have a solid grasp on how to manage file I/O in Node.js.

1. Reading Files

1.1 Using fs.readFile for Asynchronous File Reading

The simplest way to read a file in Node.js (asynchronously) is via the `fs.readFile` method.

Example: Reading a Text File

```
// readText.js
const fs = require('fs');
fs.readFile('notes.txt', 'utf8', (err, data)
=> {
  if (err) {
    return console.error('Error reading
file:', err);
  }
  console.log('File Contents:', data);
});
```

- **Explanation**:
  - We require the `fs` module (no installation needed — it's built into Node.js).

- fs.readFile('notes.txt', 'utf8', callback) reads the file contents in **UTF-8** encoding.
- If an error occurs (e.g., file not found), err will be non-null, and we log the error. Otherwise, data contains the file's contents.

1.2. Why Asynchronous?

- **Non-Blocking**: The rest of your Node.js application continues running while the file is being read.
- **Better Performance**: Asynchronous operations allow you to handle multiple tasks without waiting for I/O completion on each file read.

2. Writing Files

2.1 Using fs.writeFile to Create or Overwrite a File

fs.writeFile is an asynchronous method to create or overwrite a file.

Example: Writing to a File

```
// writeText.js
const fs = require('fs');
const content = 'Hello, this is a sample content!';
fs.writeFile('output.txt', content, (err) =>
{
  if (err) {
    return console.error('Error writing file:', err);
  }
  console.log('File has been created/overwritten with content:', content);
```

99

```
});
```

- **Explanation**:
  - `fs.writeFile('output.txt', content, callback)` creates a new file if none exists, or overwrites an existing one.
  - On success, we log a confirmation message. On error, we log the error details.

2.2. Common Use Cases

1. **Saving Application Data**: For instance, saving user input to a text file.
2. **Exporting Logs**: Writing logs or debugging information to a file.
3. **Generating Reports**: Creating a dynamic file (e.g., CSV or JSON) from application data.

3. Practical Example: Logging Requests to a File

One common use case is **logging HTTP requests** that hit your Node.js server.

Example: Simple HTTP Server that Logs Requests

```
// requestLogger.js
const http = require('http');
const fs = require('fs');
const server = http.createServer((req, res)
=> {
  // Construct a log message
  const logEntry = `${new
Date().toISOString()} - ${req.method}
${req.url}\n`;
  // Write the log to a file (append mode)
```

```
  fs.appendFile('server.log', logEntry, (err)
=> {
    if (err) {
       console.error('Failed to write to log
file:', err);
    }
  });
  // Send a response
  res.writeHead(200, { 'Content-Type':
'text/plain' });
  res.end('Request logged successfully!');
});
server.listen(3000, () => {
  console.log('Server running at
http://localhost:3000');
});
```

1. **Create an HTTP server** using the `http` module.
2. **For every request**, build a log entry that includes the timestamp, HTTP method, and URL.
3. **Use `fs.appendFile`** to add new log entries to `server.log`.
4. **Respond** with a success message.

Testing It:

Run the script:

```
node requestLogger.js
```

1. Visit `http://localhost:3000` in your browser or send requests via command line (e.g., `curl http://localhost:3000`).
2. Check `server.log` to see each new request entry appended.

10 Coding Exercises

Below are ten exercises to solidify your understanding of reading, writing, and logging with the Node.js file system. Each exercise includes:

- **Learning Objective**
- **Full Code & Explanation**
- **Outcome** (what you'll see or learn)

Feel free to adapt file names as desired.

Exercise 1: Basic File Reader

Learning Objective

- Practice using `fs.readFile` asynchronously and handling potential errors.

```
// exercise1-read.js
const fs = require('fs');
fs.readFile('exercise1.txt', 'utf8', (err,
data) => {
  if (err) {
    return console.error('Could not read
exercise1.txt:', err);
  }
  console.log('Contents of exercise1.txt:',
data);
});
```

Outcome

- The console displays the contents of `exercise1.txt` if it exists, or an error otherwise.

Explanation

- Demonstrates reading text data from a file. You can change "exercise1.txt" to any file name.

Exercise 2: Writing to a File

Learning Objective

- Create or overwrite a file using fs.writeFile.

```
// exercise2-write.js
const fs = require('fs');
const textToWrite = 'Hello, this is Exercise 2!';
fs.writeFile('exercise2.txt', textToWrite, (err) => {
  if (err) {
    return console.error('Error writing exercise2.txt:', err);
  }
  console.log('exercise2.txt has been created with the text:', textToWrite);
});
```

Outcome

- exercise2.txt is created/overwritten with the specified text.

Explanation

- Shows how to quickly create a file. If exercise2.txt already exists, it will be overwritten.

Exercise 3: Appending to a File

Learning Objective

- Use `fs.appendFile` to add data to an existing file instead of overwriting it.

```js
// exercise3-append.js
const fs = require('fs');
const newLine = `Appended on ${new
Date().toLocaleString()}\n`;
fs.appendFile('exercise3.log', newLine, (err)
=> {
  if (err) {
    return console.error('Could not append to
exercise3.log:', err);
  }
  console.log('New line appended:',
newLine.trim());
});
```

Outcome

- `exercise3.log` grows with each run, adding a timestamped line.

Explanation

- Useful for logging or accumulating data over time.

Exercise 4: Reading a JSON File

Learning Objective

- Demonstrate reading JSON data, then parsing it into a JavaScript object.

```js
// exercise4-readJSON.js
const fs = require('fs');
fs.readFile('data.json', 'utf8', (err,
jsonString) => {
```

```
  if (err) {
    return console.error('Error reading
data.json:', err);
  }
  try {
    const data = JSON.parse(jsonString);
    console.log('Parsed JSON data:', data);
  } catch (parseErr) {
    console.error('Invalid JSON format:',
parseErr);
  }
});
```

Outcome

- If data.json contains valid JSON, logs the parsed object. Otherwise, shows an error.

Explanation

- Shows that you must **stringify** data to write JSON and **parse** data to read JSON.

Exercise 5: Writing a JSON File

Learning Objective

- Create a JSON file from a JavaScript object using JSON.stringify.

```
// exercise5-writeJSON.js
const fs = require('fs');
const user = {
  name: 'John Doe',
  age: 30,
  hobbies: ['reading', 'gaming', 'coding']
};
```

```
fs.writeFile('user.json',
JSON.stringify(user, null, 2), (err) => {
  if (err) {
    return console.error('Error writing
user.json:', err);
  }
  console.log('user.json has been created:',
user);
});
```

Outcome

- A nicely formatted user.json file is created.

Explanation

- JSON.stringify(obj, null, 2) pretty-prints the JSON with 2 spaces of indentation.

Exercise 6: Renaming a File

Learning Objective

- Use fs.rename to change the name of an existing file.

```
// exercise6-rename.js
const fs = require('fs');
fs.rename('oldName.txt', 'newName.txt', (err)
=> {
  if (err) {
    return console.error('Error renaming
file:', err);
  }
  console.log('File renamed from oldName.txt
to newName.txt');
});
```

Outcome

- If `oldName.txt` exists, it becomes `newName.txt`.

Explanation

- This helps you refactor or reorganize existing files programmatically.

Exercise 7: Deleting a File

Learning Objective

- Practice removing a file using `fs.unlink`.

```
// exercise7-delete.js
const fs = require('fs');
fs.unlink('fileToDelete.txt', (err) => {
  if (err) {
    return console.error('Could not delete
file:', err);
  }
  console.log('fileToDelete.txt has been
deleted.');
});
```

Outcome

- `fileToDelete.txt` is removed from your file system, if it exists.

Explanation

- Use with caution—this operation is permanent unless you build in custom backups or checks.

Exercise 8: Basic Logging in an HTTP Server

Learning Objective

- Combine an HTTP server with file writing to log request details.

```
// exercise8-logServer.js
const http = require('http');
const fs = require('fs');
const server = http.createServer((req, res)
=> {
  const logLine = `${new
Date().toISOString()} - ${req.method}
${req.url}\n`;
  fs.appendFile('exercise8.log', logLine,
(err) => {
    if (err) {
      console.error('Failed to append log:',
err);
    }
  });
  res.writeHead(200, { 'Content-Type':
'text/plain' });
  res.end('This request has been logged to
exercise8.log');
});
server.listen(4000, () => {
  console.log('HTTP Logging Server running on
http://localhost:4000');
});
```

Outcome

- Every request to http://localhost:4000 appends a line to exercise8.log.

108

Explanation

- Demonstrates a typical real-world scenario: recording traffic or usage data to a file.

Exercise 9: Checking File Stats

Learning Objective

- Learn how to get file information (like size, creation time) using `fs.stat`.

```
// exercise9-stat.js
const fs = require('fs');
fs.stat('exercise9.log', (err, stats) => {
  if (err) {
    return console.error('Could not get stats
of exercise9.log:', err);
  }
  console.log('File Stats:', stats);
  console.log('Is file:', stats.isFile());
  console.log('Size in bytes:', stats.size);
});
```

Outcome

- Prints details about `exercise9.log`, including size in bytes and last modification time.

Explanation

- `stats` includes info such as `size`, `mtime` (modified time), and methods like `isFile()` or `isDirectory()`.

Exercise 10: Watching a File for Changes

Learning Objective

- Explore `fs.watch` to detect modifications to a file in real-time.

```
// exercise10-watch.js
const fs = require('fs');
const fileName = 'watchedFile.txt';
fs.watch(fileName, (eventType, filename) => {
  if (filename) {
    console.log(`File ${filename} changed!
Event type: ${eventType}`);
  } else {
    console.log('Filename not provided');
  }
});
// Keep the process alive
console.log(`Watching for changes in
${fileName}...`);
```

Outcome

- Whenever `watchedFile.txt` is edited and saved, the console logs a message indicating the change.

Explanation

- Useful for automatically reloading data or triggering other actions when a file updates.

10 Multiple Choice Quiz Questions

Each question below tests your knowledge of Node.js file system operations. Detailed answers follow.

1. **Which Node.js method reads a file asynchronously?**
   A. `fs.readFileSync()`
   B. `fs.readFile()`
   C. `fs.writeFile()`
   D. `fs.createReadStream()`
   Correct Answer: B. `fs.readFile()`
   Explanation:
   - `fs.readFile()` is the asynchronous method. `fs.readFileSync()` does the same but blocks the execution until finished.

2. **What is the default behavior of `fs.writeFile` if the file already exists?**
   A. It appends content to the end of the file
   B. It throws an error and does not write
   C. It overwrites the existing file content
   D. It creates a backup of the existing file, then writes
   Correct Answer: C. It overwrites the existing file content
   Explanation:
   - If the file exists, Node.js overwrites it with the new data.

3. **Which method would you use to append data to a file without overwriting its existing content?**
   A. `fs.appendFile()`
   B. `fs.modifyFile()`
   C. `fs.insertFile()`
   D. `fs.extendFile()`
   Correct Answer: A. `fs.appendFile()`
   Explanation:
   - `fs.appendFile()` adds new data at the end of an existing file, or creates it if it doesn't exist.

4. **In a Node.js HTTP server, what is a common practice for logging requests to a file?**
A. Reading all request data and storing it in an array in memory
B. Using `fs.appendFile()` in the server callback with a timestamp and request info
C. Modifying the `req` object to store logs automatically
D. Using `fs.readFile()` in every request to store logs
Correct Answer: B. Using `fs.appendFile()` in the server callback with a timestamp and request info
Explanation:
   o Appending logs to a file is typical for server-side logging. In the callback, you can gather request data and write it to disk.

5. **Which method is not part of the Node.js `fs` module?**
A. `fs.rename()`
B. `fs.unwatchFile()`
C. `fs.mkdir()`
D. `fs.httpFile()`
Correct Answer: D. `fs.httpFile()`
Explanation:
   o `fs.httpFile()` does not exist in the Node.js `fs` module. The others (`fs.rename()`, `fs.unwatchFile()`, and `fs.mkdir()`) are real methods.

6. **What parameter must you include if you want to read a text file as a string in `fs.readFile`?**
A. The `encoding`, e.g., `'utf8'`
B. The file offset
C. The method name
D. The sync flag
Correct Answer: A. The `encoding`, e.g., `'utf8'`
Explanation:
   o Passing `'utf8'` (or another encoding) ensures you get a string instead of a `Buffer`.

7. Which method is used to gather stats (like size or modified time) about a file?
   A. `fs.inspect()`
   B. `fs.stat()`
   C. `fs.review()`
   D. `fs.data()`
   Correct Answer: B. `fs.stat()`
   Explanation:
   - `fs.stat()` retrieves a `Stats` object containing information about the file.

8. If you want to rename a file from `old.txt` to `new.txt`, which method would you call?
   A. `fs.copyFile('old.txt', 'new.txt')`
   B. `fs.moveFile('old.txt', 'new.txt')`
   C. `fs.rename('old.txt', 'new.txt')`
   D. `fs.update('old.txt', 'new.txt')`
   Correct Answer: C. `fs.rename('old.txt', 'new.txt')`
   Explanation:
   - `fs.rename()` is the correct method for renaming or moving a file on the filesystem.

9. What happens if `fs.unlink()` is called on a file that does not exist?
   A. It silently creates a new file
   B. It throws an error in the callback
   C. It does nothing
   D. It calls `fs.writeFile()` to generate a backup
   Correct Answer: B. It throws an error in the callback
   Explanation:
   - Deleting a non-existent file results in an error. Always handle potential errors in the callback.

10. **Which statement about `fs.watch()` is correct?**
    A. It synchronously watches a file and blocks the thread
    B. It requires installing an external npm package
    C. It is used to monitor file changes and triggers an event on each change
    D. It can only watch directory-level changes, not files
    Correct Answer: C. It is used to monitor file changes and triggers an event on each change
    Explanation:
    - `fs.watch()` is built-in and asynchronously notifies you of changes in a file or directory.

Summary

In this chapter, you:

- **Learned to read files asynchronously** with `fs.readFile`, handling potential errors via callbacks.
- **Practiced writing files** with `fs.writeFile`, overwriting existing data if the file already exists.
- **Explored a practical example**: logging HTTP requests to a file, a common technique for tracking traffic in production.
- **Completed 10 exercises** that guide you through reading JSON, writing text, appending data, renaming, deleting, and watching files for changes.

Understanding these fundamentals of the Node.js file system module will allow you to store, retrieve, and manage data in a variety of ways. Next, you can further explore advanced file-streaming techniques, or combine your new skills with server development to build file-based APIs, logging systems, or file-management utilities.

Chapter 7. Working with Packages

As a Node.js developer, you're not limited to only using the core modules. The **Node Package Manager (npm)** ecosystem offers millions of third-party packages, enabling you to extend your application's functionality quickly. In this chapter, we'll explore how to install and use third-party packages, see an example of using **chalk** for colorful console output, and learn about **nodemon**, a useful tool that auto-restarts your server during development.

1. Installing and Using Third-Party Packages

1.1. What Is npm (Node Package Manager)?

- **npm** is the default package manager for Node.js, installed automatically when you install Node.js.
- It's used to install, update, and manage Node.js packages (often called modules or libraries).

1.2. Installing a Package Locally

To install a package locally (within your project folder), use:

```
npm install package-name
```

This creates a `node_modules` folder and adds the dependency to your `package.json` under `"dependencies"`. For example:

```
npm install chalk
```

1.3. Importing and Using a Package

Once installed, import the package in your code using CommonJS `require` or ES Modules `import`:

```
// Using CommonJS
const chalk = require('chalk');
// Using ES Modules (if your project is
configured or you use .mjs extension)
// import chalk from 'chalk';
```

After importing, you can call its methods and use its features in your scripts.

2. Example: Using chalk for Colorful Console Output

chalk is a popular library for styling strings in the terminal. It allows you to apply colors, backgrounds, and other text effects.

Installation:

```
npm install chalk
```

Usage Example:

```
// chalkExample.js
const chalk = require('chalk');
console.log(chalk.green('Hello in green
text!'));
console.log(chalk.bold.blue('Bold and blue
text!'));
console.log(chalk.red.bgWhite('Red text with
a white background!'));
```

- **Explanation**:
  - chalk.green(...) styles the text as green.

- chalk.bold.blue(...) applies both bold and blue styles.
- Each styling method can be chained together for creative terminal outputs.

When you run:

```
node chalkExample.js
```

You'll see colorful text in your terminal, depending on the chalk methods used.

3. Introduction to nodemon

nodemon is a development tool that automatically restarts your Node.js application when it detects changes in your files. This eliminates the need to stop and start your server manually after every modification.

3.1. Installing nodemon

You can install **nodemon** globally or as a dev dependency:

Globally (useful for multiple projects):

```
npm install -g nodemon
```
As a dev dependency (in one specific project):

```
npm install --save-dev nodemon
```

3.2. Using nodemon

Run your Node.js application using the nodemon command instead of node:

```
nodemon app.js
```

- **nodemon** watches all the files in the current directory (by default).
- If any watched file changes, **nodemon** restarts app.js.

3.3. Example: Server with nodemon

```
// server.js
const http = require('http');
const server = http.createServer((req, res)
=> {
  res.end('Hello from a server watched by
nodemon!');
});
server.listen(3000, () => {
  console.log('Server running at
http://localhost:3000');
});
```

Now run:

```
nodemon server.js
```

1. Visit http://localhost:3000 — you'll see your message.
2. Edit server.js (for example, change the message).
3. **nodemon** restarts the server automatically — no manual intervention needed.

10 Coding Exercises

Below are ten hands-on exercises to help you gain proficiency with npm, chalk, and nodemon. Each exercise includes:

1. **Learning Objective**
2. **Full Code & Explanation**
3. **Outcome** (what you'll see or achieve)

Exercise 1: Initializing a New Project with npm init

Learning Objective

- Practice creating a `package.json` with default values and understand its contents.

Steps

Create a new folder:

```
mkdir project-exercise1
cd project-exercise1
```

1. Run `npm init -y` to generate a default `package.json`.
2. Open `package.json` and observe the fields (name, version, scripts, etc.).

Outcome

- You'll have a `package.json` file with defaults.
- Familiarity with the sections of a typical `package.json`.

Explanation

- `npm init -y` automatically populates `package.json` with default values, speeding up initial setup.

Exercise 2: Installing and Using chalk

Learning Objective

- Learn how to install a third-party package and use it.

Install chalk:

```
npm install chalk
```

Create exercise2-chalk.js:

```
// exercise2-chalk.js
const chalk = require('chalk');
console.log(chalk.red('This text is red!'));
console.log(chalk.green('This text is
green!'));
console.log(chalk.bgBlue('This text has a
blue background!'));
```

Run the file:

```
node exercise2-chalk.js
```

Outcome

- Colored text in your terminal, demonstrating the usage of a third-party package.

Explanation

- You see how to require an npm-installed package (chalk) and apply its methods.

Exercise 3: Globally Installing nodemon

Learning Objective

- Understand how to install a package globally for system-wide usage.

Global Installation:

```
npm install -g nodemon
```

120

Verify it installed properly:

```
nodemon --version
```

1. **Explanation**:
   - ○ If you see a version number, nodemon is installed globally on your system.

Outcome

- You can now run `nodemon <filename>` from any directory without installing it per project.

Explanation

- `-g` or `--global` installs nodemon outside the scope of a single project, letting you use it anywhere.

Exercise 4: Using nodemon in a Local Project

Learning Objective

- Install **nodemon** as a dev dependency and set up a script to use it.

Local Installation:

```
npm install --save-dev nodemon
```
Add a script in `package.json`:

```json
{
  "scripts": {
    "start": "node app.js",
    "dev": "nodemon app.js"
  }
}
```

1. **Outcome**:

- You can now run npm run dev to start your app with **nodemon**.

Explanation

- This method is more common when distributing a project, so others can run dev scripts without installing nodemon globally.

Exercise 5: Colorful Logging with chalk

Learning Objective

- Combine chalk with a simple HTTP server to log color-coded messages.

```
// exercise5-colorServer.js
const http = require('http');
const chalk = require('chalk');
const server = http.createServer((req, res)
=> {
  console.log(chalk.blue(`Received request:
${req.method} ${req.url}`));
  res.end('Check your console for a colorful
log!');
});
server.listen(3005, () => {
  console.log(chalk.green('Server running at
http://localhost:3005'));
});
```

1. **Run** node exercise5-colorServer.js (or nodemon if you prefer).
2. **Visit** http://localhost:3005 in your browser.

Outcome

- Logs incoming requests in blue.
- Logs the server start message in green.

Explanation

- Demonstrates how chalk can help highlight different messages (e.g., errors in red, success in green).

Exercise 6: Creating a Custom npm Script

Learning Objective

- Practice adding a script to run **chalk** examples directly from `package.json`.

In your project's `package.json`, add:

```
{
  "scripts": {
    "show-colors": "node exercise2-chalk.js"
  }
}
```
Run:

```
npm run show-colors
```

1. **Outcome**
   - The terminal outputs your chalk-colored text as defined in `exercise2-chalk.js`.

Explanation

- npm scripts allow you to define shortcuts for repetitive commands.

Exercise 7: Exploring npm outdated and npm update

Learning Objective

- Understand how to check for outdated dependencies and update them.

In your project folder (with dependencies installed), run:

```
npm outdated
```

1. Observe which packages are outdated.

Update specific packages:

```
npm update chalk
```

2. **Outcome**
   - Packages with newer versions are updated to the latest minor/patch versions (not a major version update unless you allow it).

Explanation

- Keeping packages updated ensures you have security patches and bug fixes.

Exercise 8: Using nodemon for a File-Watching Script

Learning Objective

- Demonstrate how **nodemon** can watch non-HTTP scripts.

```
// exercise8-counter.js
let count = 0;
setInterval(() => {
```

```
  count++;
  console.log(`Counter: ${count}`);
}, 1000);
```

1. **Run** nodemon exercise8-counter.js.
2. **Modify** the script (e.g., change the text). Watch nodemon restart automatically.

Outcome

- The script increments every second. Any file changes restart it automatically.

Explanation

- **nodemon** isn't limited to web servers; it can watch any Node.js script.

Exercise 9: Installing and Using Another Package (e.g., axios)

Learning Objective

- Practice installing a popular HTTP client and making a request.

Install:

```
npm install axios
```
Create exercise9-axios.js:

```
const axios = require('axios');
axios.get('https://jsonplaceholder.typicode.com/posts/1')
  .then(response => {
    console.log('Data received:',
response.data);
  })
```

```
.catch(error => {
  console.error('Error fetching data:',
error);
  });
```
Run:

```
node exercise9-axios.js
```

Outcome

- Fetches a sample JSON post from
  jsonplaceholder.typicode.com.
- Logs the data to your console.

Explanation

- Demonstrates installing a popular library (axios) and making a GET request in Node.js.

Exercise 10: Uninstalling a Package

Learning Objective

- Learn how to remove packages that are no longer needed.

Uninstall a package (e.g., chalk):

```
npm uninstall chalk
```

1. **Observe** your package.json and node_modules folder:
   - chalk is removed from both.

Outcome

- chalk is no longer available, and any scripts requiring it will fail.

Explanation

- Uninstalling frees space and avoids confusion when packages are no longer necessary.

10 Multiple Choice Quiz Questions

Below are ten questions to test your understanding of working with packages in Node.js. Each question has a detailed explanation.

1. **Which command creates a basic `package.json` with default values in the current directory?**
   A. `npm install`
   B. `npm init`
   C. `npm init -y`
   D. `npm new package.json`
   Answer: C. `npm init -y`
   Explanation:
      - `npm init -y` automatically accepts default answers for `package.json` fields.
2. **If you install a package locally, where is it stored by default?**
   A. In the `.npm` folder in your user directory
   B. In a `lib` folder in your Node.js installation
   C. In the `node_modules` folder within your project
   D. Globally in your system's PATH
   Answer: C. In the `node_modules` folder within your project
   Explanation:
      - A local install places dependencies in `node_modules` relative to your project's root directory.

3. **What is not true about using** `npm install -g package-name`**?**
A. It installs the package globally
B. You can use the package commands from any folder
C. It adds the package to your project's `package.json` as a dependency
D. You typically use this for CLI tools
Answer: C. It adds the package to your project's `package.json` as a dependency
Explanation:
   o Installing globally does **not** update your local `package.json`. It makes the package available system-wide.

4. **Which command is used to run a Node.js script using nodemon?**
A. `node nodemon app.js`
B. `npm run nodemon`
C. `nodemon app.js`
D. `start nodemon app.js`
Answer: C. `nodemon app.js`
Explanation:
   o Once nodemon is installed (globally or locally), you can run `nodemon <filename>` to automatically restart on file changes.

5. **What is the primary purpose of nodemon?**
A. To install dependencies listed in `package.json`
B. To automatically restart your Node.js application when files change
C. To create a production build of your Node.js server
D. To lock down dependency versions
Answer: B. To automatically restart your Node.js application when files change
Explanation:
   o nodemon monitors your project files, restarting the process upon changes, thus speeding up development.

6. **Which of the following is a chalk usage example?**
   A. `const chalk = require('chalk');`
   `console.log(chalk.green('Green text'));`
   B. `import chalk from 'chalk';`
   `console.log(chalk(format='green')('Green`
   `text'));`
   C. `require('chalk');`
   `chalk.setColor('green');`
   `console.log('Green text');`
   D. `npm chalk -color=green -print 'Green`
   `text'`
   Answer: A
   Explanation:
   - `chalk.green(...)` is the conventional way.
     Option B is partially correct for ES Modules, but
     `chalk(format='green')` is incorrect usage.
     Option C and D are invalid.

7. **If you want to define a custom script in your package.json named "dev" that runs nodemon app.js, which snippet is correct?**
   A. `{"scripts":{"dev":"nodemon app.js"`
   `}}`
   B. `{"custom": {"dev": "nodemon app.js"`
   `}}`
   C. `{"scripts": "nodemon app.js"}`
   D. `{"scripts": { "dev":["nodemon`
   `app.js"]      }}`
   Answer: A
   Explanation:
   - The `"scripts"` section in `package.json` is
     where you define commands. A is the correct
     format, as the value of the script should be a
     string.

8. **What is the correct way to uninstall a package named "lodash"?**

   A. `npm remove --force lodash`

   B. `npm uninstall lodash`

   C. `rm -rf node_modules/lodash`

   D. `npm delete lodash`

   Answer: B. `npm uninstall lodash`

   Explanation:
   - `npm uninstall <package>` is the official command for removing a dependency.

9. **Which command checks for packages that are out of date in your project?**

   A. `npm outdated`

   B. `npm info`

   C. `npm list --updates`

   D. `npm checkVersions`

   Answer: A. `npm outdated`

   Explanation:
   - `npm outdated` lists any packages that have newer versions in the npm registry.

10. **If you install chalk without specifying `--save` or `--save-dev`, what happens in the latest npm versions?**

    A. Nothing is installed unless you specify `--save`

    B. It installs globally by default

    C. It is installed locally and added to `dependencies` in `package.json`

    D. It creates a lockfile but no `package.json` entry

    Answer: C. It is installed locally and added to `dependencies` in `package.json`

    Explanation:
    - As of npm v5 and above, installing a package (e.g., `npm install chalk`) automatically adds it to `dependencies`.

Summary

1. **Installing Third-Party Packages**
   - You can use `npm install <package>` to add external modules to your project's `node_modules` folder.
   - Import them in your code using `require` (CommonJS) or `import` (ES modules).
2. **Using chalk**
   - A library for coloring and styling text in the terminal.
   - Great for making logs or CLI outputs more readable.
3. **nodemon**
   - Automatically restarts Node.js applications on file changes, boosting development efficiency.
   - Install globally or locally, then run your files with `nodemon <file>`.

By completing the coding exercises and quizzes, you've gained real-world practice installing, removing, updating, and utilizing third-party packages. You're now ready to incorporate more specialized libraries and tools into your Node.js applications, streamline your development workflow with **nodemon**, and produce more visually appealing console outputs with **chalk**.

Chapter 8. Introduction to Asynchronous Programming

Asynchronous programming is a core concept in Node.js, allowing your application to perform tasks in parallel rather than waiting for each operation to complete before moving on to the next. This section will cover the fundamental tools for writing asynchronous code in Node.js:

1. **Callbacks** – The original style of async programming, using functions passed as parameters.
2. **Promises** – An evolution that helps avoid "callback hell" by chaining `.then` and `.catch` methods.
3. **Async/Await** – A modern syntax that makes asynchronous code look and behave more like synchronous code.

By the end of this chapter, you'll be able to handle asynchronous operations using each of these approaches, choose which style fits your project, and understand how to handle errors effectively.

1. Callbacks

In JavaScript (and Node.js), a **callback** is a function passed as an argument to another function. When the asynchronous work finishes, the callback is invoked, passing any result or error.

1.1. Basic Example of a Callback Function

```
// callbackExample.js
function getUserData(userId, callback) {
  // Simulate an asynchronous operation with
setTimeout
  setTimeout(() => {
    const user = { id: userId, name: "Alice"
};
    callback(null, user); // (error, result)
  }, 1000);
}
console.log("Before getUserData call...");
getUserData(42, (err, user) => {
  if (err) {
    return console.error("Error:", err);
```

```
  }
  console.log("User received:", user);
});
console.log("After getUserData call...");
```

- **Explanation**:
  - ○ getUserData simulates an async operation via setTimeout.
  - ○ After 1 second, we invoke callback(null, user).
  - ○ callback(null, user) means "no error, here is your user data."
  - ○ If an error occurred, we'd call callback(err, null) instead.
- **Key Takeaway**: The main thread doesn't block or pause for the data; it continues running other code in the meantime.

2. Promises

Promises are a more modern approach to handling async tasks, introduced to solve the "callback hell" issue. A **Promise** object represents a value that may be available now, later, or never.

2.1. Understanding .then and .catch

A promise can be in one of three states:

- **Pending**: The initial state
- **Fulfilled**: The operation completed successfully (triggers .then)
- **Rejected**: The operation failed (triggers .catch)

Example:

```
// promiseExample.js
```

```javascript
function getUserDataPromise(userId) {
  return new Promise((resolve, reject) => {
    setTimeout(() => {
      // Simulated success scenario
      if (userId > 0) {
        resolve({ id: userId, name: "Bob" });
      } else {
        reject("Invalid user ID");
      }
    }, 1000);
  });
}
console.log("Before getUserDataPromise
call...");
getUserDataPromise(10)
  .then((user) => {
    console.log("Promise resolved with
user:", user);
  })
  .catch((error) => {
    console.error("Promise rejected with
error:", error);
  });
console.log("After getUserDataPromise
call...");
```

- **Explanation**:
    - resolve is called if the async operation is successful, passing the fulfilled value.
    - reject is called if the operation fails, passing an error message or object.
    - .then handles a fulfilled promise, .catch handles a rejected one.

3. Async/Await

Async/Await is syntactic sugar built on top of Promises. Instead of chaining `.then` and `.catch`, you write code that **appears** synchronous but is still asynchronous under the hood.

3.1. Simplifying Asynchronous Code

```js
// asyncAwaitExample.js
function getUserDataPromise(userId) {
  return new Promise((resolve, reject) => {
    setTimeout(() => {
      if (userId > 0) {
        resolve({ id: userId, name: "Charlie"
});
      } else {
        reject("Invalid user ID");
      }
    }, 1000);
  });
}
async function showUserData() {
  try {
    console.log("Before awaiting user
data...");
    const user = await getUserDataPromise(5);
    console.log("Async/Await User:", user);
    console.log("After awaiting user
data...");
  } catch (err) {
    console.error("Caught an error:", err);
  }
}
showUserData();
```

- **Explanation**:
  - The `async` keyword on `showUserData` allows the use of `await` inside.
  - `await getUserDataPromise(5)` waits for the promise to be resolved or rejected.
  - If an error occurs, it's caught by the `try/catch` block.
  - This style is more readable, especially when you have multiple sequential async calls.

10 Coding Exercises

Below are ten exercises that reinforce the concepts of callbacks, promises, and async/await. Each exercise includes:

- **Learning Objective**
- **Full Code**
- **Outcome**
- **Explanation**

Feel free to rename files or adapt the code as needed.

Exercise 1: Simple Callback with setTimeout

Learning Objective: Understand how a callback is used with a simulated delay.

```
// exercise1-callback.js
function delayedMessage(message, callback) {
  setTimeout(() => {
    callback(`Received message: ${message}`);
  }, 500);
}
console.log("Start...");
delayedMessage("Hello Callback!", (result) =>
{
```

```
    console.log(result);
});
console.log("End...");
```

Outcome:

Prints:

```
Start...
End...
Received message: Hello Callback!
```

- Notice the "End..." logs before the callback finishes.

Explanation:

- Shows how the main flow continues while setTimeout runs in the background, then fires the callback after 500ms.

Exercise 2: Callback Error Handling

Learning Objective: Implement error handling in a callback pattern.

```
// exercise2-callbackError.js
function fetchUserData(userId, callback) {
  setTimeout(() => {
    if (userId > 0) {
      callback(null, { id: userId, name:
"Diana" });
    } else {
      callback("User ID must be positive",
null);
    }
  }, 700);
}
```

```
fetchUserData(-1, (err, data) => {
  if (err) {
    return console.error("Error in
callback:", err);
  }
  console.log("User data:", data);
});
```

Outcome:

- If userId is negative or zero, logs "Error in callback: User ID must be positive."

Explanation:

- Demonstrates the Node.js convention: (error, data) signature. The first argument is an error or null.

Exercise 3: Converting a Callback to a Promise

Learning Objective: Transform callback-based code into a promise-based function.

```
// exercise3-promiseConversion.js
function fetchDataCallback(callback) {
  setTimeout(() => {
    callback(null, "Callback data");
  }, 500);
}
// Convert the above function to return a
Promise
function fetchDataPromise() {
  return new Promise((resolve, reject) => {
    fetchDataCallback((err, data) => {
      if (err) return reject(err);
      resolve(data);
```

```
    });
  });
}
// Test the promise
fetchDataPromise()
  .then((result) => {
    console.log("Promise result:", result);
  })
  .catch((err) => {
    console.error("Promise error:", err);
  });
```

Outcome:

- Logs "Promise result: Callback data" after 500ms.

Explanation:

- This shows how to wrap callback-based APIs in a promise, enabling `.then`/`.catch` usage.

Exercise 4: Promise Chain

Learning Objective: Use `.then` chaining to perform sequential async operations.

```
// exercise4-promiseChain.js
function stepOne() {
  return new Promise((resolve) => {
    setTimeout(() => resolve("Step One
Complete"), 300);
  });
}
function stepTwo(prevMessage) {
  return new Promise((resolve) => {
    setTimeout(() => resolve(`${prevMessage},
Step Two Complete`), 300);
```
139

```
  });
}
function stepThree(prevMessage) {
  return new Promise((resolve) => {
    setTimeout(() => resolve(`${prevMessage},
Step Three Complete`), 300);
  });
}
stepOne()
  .then((msg1) => stepTwo(msg1))
  .then((msg2) => stepThree(msg2))
  .then((finalMsg) => {
    console.log("All steps done:", finalMsg);
  })
  .catch((err) => console.error("Error:",
err));
```

Outcome:

After ~900ms, logs:

```
All steps done: Step One Complete, Step Two
Complete, Step Three Complete
```

Explanation:

- Shows how you can chain multiple async tasks in a sequence with promises.

Exercise 5: Promise Error Handling

Learning Objective: Demonstrate .catch to handle rejections.

```
// exercise5-promiseError.js
function riskyOperation() {
  return new Promise((resolve, reject) => {
```

```javascript
  setTimeout(() => {
    const success = Math.random() > 0.5; //
50% chance
    if (success) {
      resolve("Operation succeeded!");
    } else {
      reject("Operation failed!");
    }
  }, 400);
  });
}
riskyOperation()
  .then((msg) => console.log(msg))
  .catch((err) => console.error("Error in
promise:", err));
```

Outcome:

- Half the time, logs "Operation succeeded!"; half the time, logs "Error in promise: Operation failed!"

Explanation:

- Demonstrates how promises can cleanly handle success vs. failure scenarios.

Exercise 6: Basic async/await Example

Learning Objective: Convert promise-based code into async/await.

```javascript
// exercise6-asyncAwait.js
function getData() {
  return new Promise((resolve) => {
    setTimeout(() => resolve("Data
retrieved"), 300);
  });
```

```
}
async function showData() {
  console.log("Starting async function...");
  const result = await getData();
  console.log("Result from getData:",
result);
  console.log("Async function complete.");
}
showData();
```

Outcome:

- Logs the steps in order, highlighting that the code reads like synchronous logic but runs asynchronously.

Explanation:

- `await` only works inside an `async` function, ensuring the promise is resolved before the next line executes.

Exercise 7: Handling Errors with async/await and try/catch

Learning Objective: Understand error handling in `async`/`await` syntax.

```
// exercise7-asyncAwaitError.js
function mightFail() {
  return new Promise((resolve, reject) => {
    setTimeout(() => {
      reject("Something went wrong!");
    }, 400);
  });
}
async function handleAsyncError() {
  try {
    const data = await mightFail();
```

```
    console.log("This will never print:",
data);
  } catch (error) {
    console.error("Caught error in
async/await:", error);
  }
}
handleAsyncError();
```

Outcome:

- Logs "Caught error in async/await: Something went wrong!"

Explanation:

- The `try/catch` block captures the rejection from the promise.

Exercise 8: Using Promise.all with async/await

Learning Objective: Run multiple promises in parallel and wait for all to complete.

```
// exercise8-promiseAll.js
function createPromise(value, delay) {
  return new Promise((resolve) => {
    setTimeout(() => resolve(value), delay);
  });
}
async function parallelExecution() {
  const [res1, res2, res3] = await
Promise.all([
    createPromise("Result 1", 500),
    createPromise("Result 2", 300),
    createPromise("Result 3", 700),
  ]);
```

```
  console.log("All results:", res1, res2,
res3);
}
parallelExecution();
```

Outcome:

After ~700ms (the longest delay), logs:

```
All results: Result 1 Result 2 Result 3
```

Explanation:

- The promises run simultaneously. `Promise.all` waits for all to resolve or any to reject.

Exercise 9: Using Promise.race

Learning Objective: Learn how to retrieve the result of whichever promise resolves (or rejects) first.

```
// exercise9-promiseRace.js
function quickTask() {
  return new Promise((resolve) => {
    setTimeout(() => resolve("Quick Task
Finished!"), 200);
  });
}
function slowTask() {
  return new Promise((resolve) => {
    setTimeout(() => resolve("Slow Task
Finished!"), 600);
  });
}
Promise.race([quickTask(), slowTask()])
  .then((result) => {
    console.log("Race winner:", result);
```

```
})
.catch((error) => {
  console.error("Race error:", error);
});
```

Outcome:

- Logs "Race winner: Quick Task Finished!" because `quickTask` finishes first at 200ms.

Explanation:

- `Promise.race` resolves or rejects as soon as the first promise in the array settles.

Exercise 10: Throttling Operations with a Delay Function

Learning Objective: Combine `async/await` with a small "delay" utility function for controlling pacing.

```
// exercise10-delay.js
function delay(ms) {
  return new Promise((resolve) =>
setTimeout(resolve, ms));
}
async function doTasksWithDelay() {
  console.log("Starting tasks...");
  await delay(500);
  console.log("Task 1 complete");
  await delay(500);
  console.log("Task 2 complete");
  await delay(500);
  console.log("Task 3 complete");
  console.log("All tasks done");
}
doTasksWithDelay();
```

Outcome:

- Logs the tasks in sequence with 500ms gaps.

Explanation:

- A `delay` function is often handy to control or simulate slow operations in asynchronous code.

10 Multiple Choice Quiz Questions

Each question includes a detailed explanation of the correct answer.

1. **In Node.js, which approach is not commonly used for asynchronous programming?**
   A. Callbacks
   B. Promises
   C. Async/Await
   D. Blocking loops
   Answer: D. Blocking loops
   Explanation:
   - Callbacks, Promises, and Async/Await are standard async patterns. A blocking loop halts Node.js's single thread, which goes against its non-blocking design.
2. **What is the main advantage of using Promises over raw callbacks?**
   A. Promises make code run faster
   B. Promises automatically retry failed operations
   C. Promises allow chaining and structured error handling
   D. Promises do not require `then` or `catch`
   Answer: C. Promises allow chaining and structured error handling
   Explanation:

- Promises mitigate "callback hell" by providing `.then` and `.catch`, leading to cleaner flow and error handling.

3. **Which statement about `async`/`await` is true?**

   A. `await` blocks the entire Node.js process until the promise resolves

   B. `await` can only be used inside functions declared with `async`

   C. `await` is slower than using `.then`

   D. `async` is used for synchronous code only

   Answer: B. `await` can only be used inside functions declared with `async`

   Explanation:
   - JavaScript enforces that `await` may only appear inside an `async` function (or a top-level body in ES modules with certain flags). It doesn't block the entire process; it suspends that function's execution.

4. **In a callback function signature (`error, result`) `=> {...}`, the first argument usually represents:**

   A. The success value

   B. The resolved promise

   C. The error object (if any)

   D. The promise ID

   Answer: C. The error object (if any)

   Explanation:
   - The Node.js callback pattern is (`err, data`). If `err` is not null, an error occurred; otherwise `data` is your result.

5. Which code snippet correctly creates and returns a new Promise?

A. `return Promise.resolve((resolve, reject) => { ... });`

B. `return new Promise((resolve, reject) => { ... });`

C. `return new promise((res, rej) => { ... });`

D. `return create new Promise((resolve, reject) => { ... });`

Answer: B. `return new Promise((resolve, reject) => { ... });`

Explanation:

- The standard syntax is `new Promise((resolve, reject) => { ... })`.

6. If you have a promise chain, where do you handle any potential error that arises in any of the `.then` calls?

A. Only in the first `.then`

B. Only in the last `.then`

C. In a `.catch` block at the end of the chain

D. You cannot handle errors in promise chains

Answer: C. In a `.catch` block at the end of the chain

Explanation:

- One `.catch` at the end can catch rejections thrown by any promise in the chain.

7. What happens if an error is thrown inside an `async` function and is not caught by a try/catch?

A. It becomes a rejected promise

B. It is silently ignored

C. It automatically retries the operation

D. It blocks the event loop

Answer: A. It becomes a rejected promise

Explanation:

○ Unhandled errors in async functions translate into rejections, which can be handled with `.catch` on the returned promise or a try/catch block inside the function.

8. **Which is not a valid state of a JavaScript promise?**
A. Pending
B. Fulfilled
C. Canceled
D. Rejected
Answer: C. Canceled
Explanation:
○ JavaScript promises do not have a "canceled" state. The official states are pending, fulfilled, and rejected.

9. **In the following snippet, what will happen?**
```
async function test() {  throw
"Oops!";}test().then(() =>
console.log("Resolved")).catch(err =>
console.log("Caught:", err));
```

A. Logs "Resolved"
B. Logs "Caught: Oops!"
C. Nothing is logged
D. Logs "Oops!" and then throws an unhandled error
Answer: B. Logs "Caught: Oops!"
Explanation:

○ Throwing in an `async` function turns into a rejected promise. The `.catch` handles it.

10. **Why might you use `Promise.all` in your code?**
A. To run async tasks in strict sequence
B. To run multiple promises in parallel and only proceed when all are resolved
C. To automatically handle errors in callbacks
D. To convert a promise chain into a callback
Answer: B. To run multiple promises in parallel and only proceed when all are resolved
Explanation:

- $\circ$ `Promise.all` awaits every promise in the array. If all succeed, it fulfills with an array of results; if any fails, it rejects immediately.

Summary

Key Points:

1. **Callbacks**:
   - $\circ$ Traditional mechanism for async tasks in Node.js.
   - $\circ$ Prone to "callback hell" if nesting is excessive.
   - $\circ$ Use error-first conventions (e.g., `(err, data) => {...}`).
2. **Promises**:
   - $\circ$ Improve readability by chaining `.then` and `.catch`.
   - $\circ$ Clearer error handling, supporting multiple sequences (e.g., `Promise.all`, `Promise.race`).
3. **Async/Await**:
   - $\circ$ Syntactic sugar over promises, making async code look like synchronous code.
   - $\circ$ Use `try/catch` to handle errors.
   - $\circ$ Greatly improves code clarity in complex async workflows.

By working through the 10 exercises and quiz questions, you've gained practical experience in writing callback-based code, transitioning to promises, and finally adopting `async/await` for a cleaner style. This foundation is essential for building robust, non-blocking Node.js applications.

Chapter 9. Creating a Simple API

Building an **API (Application Programming Interface)** is a common task in Node.js development. An API allows different software systems to communicate with each other, exchanging data in a structured way. In this chapter, we'll briefly define what an API is, introduce **RESTful** APIs, explain key HTTP methods (GET and POST), and then walk through creating a basic API endpoint that serves JSON data. You'll also learn how to test your API using tools like Postman or simple browser `fetch` requests.

1. What is an API?

- **API**: A structured way for different pieces of software to interact.
- **In Web Context**: Often refers to endpoints (URLs) that allow a client to send requests and receive responses, usually in JSON format.
- **Why APIs?**: They enable separation of concerns. Front-end apps (web or mobile) can fetch data from these endpoints without depending on direct database access.

2. Introduction to RESTful APIs

A **RESTful API** (short for REpresentational State Transfer) is a style of architecture for designing networked applications. Some key principles of RESTful APIs:

1. **Client-Server**: The client (e.g., browser, mobile app) and server (API) are separated concerns.
2. **Stateless**: Each request from the client to the server must contain all the information needed to understand and process the request.

3. **Resource-based**: Data and functionality are considered as "resources" accessed via unique URLs.
4. **Use of HTTP Methods**: Commonly used methods are GET, POST, PUT, PATCH, and DELETE, each representing an action on a resource.

3. Explanation of HTTP Methods (GET, POST)

1. **GET**: Retrieve data from the server (e.g., fetch a list of items or a single item).
2. **POST**: Send data to the server to create a new resource.
3. **PUT/PATCH** (not covered in depth here): Update an existing resource.
4. **DELETE** (not covered here): Remove a resource.

In this section, we'll focus on GET and POST.

4. Building a Basic API Endpoint

We'll create a simple Node.js server with two endpoints:

1. **GET /api/users**: Returns a list of users in JSON.
2. **POST /api/users**: Accepts user data in the request body and adds it to a list.

Example:

```
// basicApi.js
const http = require('http');
let users = [
  { id: 1, name: 'Alice' },
  { id: 2, name: 'Bob' }
];
const server = http.createServer((req, res)
=> {
  // Parse URL and method
```

```javascript
  if (req.url === '/api/users' && req.method
=== 'GET') {
    // Return JSON list of users
    res.writeHead(200, { 'Content-Type':
'application/json' });
    res.end(JSON.stringify(users));
  } else if (req.url === '/api/users' &&
req.method === 'POST') {
    // Collect data from request body
    let body = '';
    req.on('data', chunk => {
      body += chunk;
    });
    req.on('end', () => {
      const newUser = JSON.parse(body);
      newUser.id = users.length + 1; //
simple ID assignment
      users.push(newUser);
      res.writeHead(201, { 'Content-Type':
'application/json' });
      res.end(JSON.stringify(newUser));
    });
  } else {
    // 404 if no route matches
    res.writeHead(404, { 'Content-Type':
'text/plain' });
    res.end('Not Found');
  }
});
server.listen(3000, () => {
  console.log('API Server running at
http://localhost:3000');
});
```

5. Testing the API

1. **Using Postman**
   - **GET** `http://localhost:3000/api/users` to see the JSON list of users.
   - **POST** `http://localhost:3000/api/users` with a JSON body like `{"name": "Charlie"}` to create a new user.
2. **Using Browser fetch**

Open your browser's console (e.g., Chrome DevTools) and type:

```
fetch('http://localhost:3000/api/users')
  .then(response => response.json())
  .then(data => console.log(data));
```

   - Or use the **Fetch** API to POST (only if you have a web page served over something like a local server at a suitable address, else CORS might apply).

10 Coding Exercises

Below are ten exercises that build on creating, testing, and expanding a simple API. Each exercise includes:

1. **Learning Objective**
2. **Full Code**
3. **Outcome**
4. **Explanation**

Feel free to modify endpoints or data structures as you like.

Exercise 1: Simple GET Endpoint

Learning Objective

- Set up a Node.js server that returns a hard-coded JSON object when a user sends a GET request.

```
// exercise1-get.js
const http = require('http');
const server = http.createServer((req, res)
=> {
  if (req.url === '/api/hello' && req.method
=== 'GET') {
    const data = { message: 'Hello, API!' };
    res.writeHead(200, { 'Content-Type':
'application/json' });
    res.end(JSON.stringify(data));
  } else {
    res.writeHead(404);
    res.end();
  }
});
server.listen(3001, () => {
  console.log('Server running at
http://localhost:3001');
});
```

Outcome

- Visiting http://localhost:3001/api/hello returns {"message": "Hello, API!"}.

Explanation

- Demonstrates the simplest GET endpoint responding with JSON data.

Exercise 2: Handling Query Strings in GET Requests

Learning Objective

- Parse query parameters in a URL (e.g., ?name=John).

```
// exercise2-query.js
const http = require('http');
const url = require('url');
const server = http.createServer((req, res)
=> {
  if (req.method === 'GET') {
    const parsedUrl = url.parse(req.url,
true); // parse with query
    if (parsedUrl.pathname === '/api/greet')
{
      const name = parsedUrl.query.name ||
'Stranger';
      const data = { greeting: `Hello,
${name}!` };
      res.writeHead(200, { 'Content-Type':
'application/json' });
      return res.end(JSON.stringify(data));
    }
  }
  res.writeHead(404);
  res.end();
});
server.listen(3002, () => {
  console.log('Server running at
http://localhost:3002');
});
```

Outcome

- `http://localhost:3002/api/greet?name=Ali ce` returns `{"greeting": "Hello, Alice!"}`.

Explanation

- Node's built-in `url.parse` (or the newer URL object) can handle query strings.

Exercise 3: Basic POST Endpoint

Learning Objective

- Accept JSON in the request body using Node's `data` and `end` events.

```
// exercise3-post.js
const http = require('http');
const server = http.createServer((req, res)
=> {
  if (req.url === '/api/data' && req.method
=== 'POST') {
    let body = '';
    req.on('data', (chunk) => {
      body += chunk;
    });
    req.on('end', () => {
      const received = JSON.parse(body);
      const response = {
        status: 'success',
        received
      };
      res.writeHead(201, { 'Content-Type':
'application/json' });
      res.end(JSON.stringify(response));
    });
  } else {
```

```
      res.writeHead(404);
      res.end();
  }
});
server.listen(3003, () => {
  console.log('Server running at
http://localhost:3003');
});
```

Outcome

- Sending a POST request (e.g., via Postman) with JSON body { "test": 123 } returns { "status": "success", "received": { "test": 123 } }.

Explanation

- Showcases how to parse incoming JSON data and respond accordingly.

Exercise 4: Managing an In-Memory Array of Items

Learning Objective

- Create GET and POST endpoints to list and add items to an array stored in memory.

```
// exercise4-items.js
const http = require('http');
let items = [];
const server = http.createServer((req, res)
=> {
  if (req.url === '/api/items' && req.method
=== 'GET') {
    res.writeHead(200, { 'Content-Type':
'application/json' });
```

```
      res.end(JSON.stringify(items));
  } else if (req.url === '/api/items' &&
req.method === 'POST') {
    let body = '';
    req.on('data', chunk => (body += chunk));
    req.on('end', () => {
      const newItem = JSON.parse(body);
      items.push(newItem);
      res.writeHead(201, { 'Content-Type':
'application/json' });
      res.end(JSON.stringify(newItem));
    });
  } else {
    res.writeHead(404);
    res.end();
  }
});
server.listen(3004, () => {
  console.log('Items API on
http://localhost:3004');
});
```

Outcome

- GET /api/items: Returns the current array.
- POST /api/items: Adds a new item to the in-memory list.

Explanation

- Demonstrates how to maintain simple state within a Node.js server (not persisted to disk).

Exercise 5: Custom Status Codes and Headers

Learning Objective

159

- Set custom response headers and status codes for different outcomes.

```
// exercise5-customStatus.js
const http = require('http');
const server = http.createServer((req, res)
=> {
  if (req.url === '/api/check' && req.method
=== 'GET') {
    // Example: return 202 Accepted with a
custom header
    res.writeHead(202, {
      'Content-Type': 'application/json',
      'X-Custom-Header': 'APICheck'
    });
    res.end(JSON.stringify({ message:
'Accepted for processing' }));
  } else {
    res.writeHead(404, { 'Content-Type':
'text/plain' });
    res.end('Route not found');
  }
});
server.listen(3005, () => {
  console.log('Custom status server at
http://localhost:3005');
});
```

Outcome

- Sends a 202 status, X-Custom-Header, and JSON response for /api/check.

Explanation

- Helps you learn to customize responses to suit various HTTP scenarios.

Exercise 6: Querying an In-Memory Dataset with GET

Learning Objective

- Filter an in-memory array based on query parameters (e.g., search by name).

```
// exercise6-filter.js
const http = require('http');
const url = require('url');
let products = [
  { id: 1, name: 'Notebook' },
  { id: 2, name: 'Laptop' },
  { id: 3, name: 'Pen' },
  { id: 4, name: 'Pencil' }
];
const server = http.createServer((req, res)
=> {
  if (req.method === 'GET') {
    const parsedUrl = url.parse(req.url,
true);
    if (parsedUrl.pathname ===
'/api/products') {
      const search = parsedUrl.query.search
|| '';
      const filtered = products.filter((p) =>

p.name.toLowerCase().includes(search.toLowerC
ase())
      );
      res.writeHead(200, { 'Content-Type':
'application/json' });
      return
res.end(JSON.stringify(filtered));
    }
  }
```

```
    res.writeHead(404);
    res.end();
});
server.listen(3006, () => {
  console.log('Product filter server at
http://localhost:3006');
});
```

Outcome

- GET /api/products?search=pen returns items
  with "pen" in their name (Pen and Pencil).

Explanation

- Demonstrates dynamic GET requests and data filtering
  on the server side.

Exercise 7: Return Error Response for Missing Fields (POST)

Learning Objective

- Validate the JSON body in a POST request and return
  an error if required fields are missing.

```
// exercise7-validation.js
const http = require('http');
const server = http.createServer((req, res)
=> {
  if (req.url === '/api/users' && req.method
=== 'POST') {
    let body = '';
    req.on('data', (chunk) => (body +=
chunk));
    req.on('end', () => {
      const parsed = JSON.parse(body);
```

```javascript
    if (!parsed.name) {
        res.writeHead(400, { 'Content-Type':
'application/json' });
        return res.end(JSON.stringify({
error: 'Name is required' }));
      }
      // Otherwise, success
      res.writeHead(201, { 'Content-Type':
'application/json' });
      res.end(JSON.stringify({ status: 'User
created', user: parsed }));
    });
  } else {
    res.writeHead(404);
    res.end();
  }
});
server.listen(3007, () => {
  console.log('Validation server running at
http://localhost:3007');
});
```

Outcome

- POSTing {"name":"Eve"} yields
  {"status":"User
  created","user":{"name":"Eve"}}.
- Missing name => 400 error with {"error":"Name
  is required"}.

Explanation

- Showcases how to handle invalid or incomplete data
  from the client.

Exercise 8: Using Node's http vs. express (Comparison Exercise)

Learning Objective

- Compare raw `http` handling to a simple Express-style approach (though we won't rely on the full Express framework here—just a conceptual look).

```
// exercise8-compare.js
// This example won't use Express, but let's
show how you'd do it differently.
const http = require('http');
// Raw Node HTTP server example
const rawServer = http.createServer((req,
res) => {
  if (req.url === '/api/raw' && req.method
=== 'GET') {
    res.writeHead(200, { 'Content-Type':
'application/json' });
    return res.end(JSON.stringify({ message:
'Raw Node.js route' }));
  }
  res.writeHead(404);
  res.end();
});
rawServer.listen(3008, () => {
  console.log('Raw server at
http://localhost:3008');
});
/*
// Hypothetical Express usage (not fully
executed here):
const express = require('express');
const app = express();
app.get('/api/express', (req, res) => {
  res.json({ message: 'Express route' });
```

```
});
app.listen(3009, () => {
  console.log('Express server at
http://localhost:3009');
});
*/
```

Outcome

- Observing code helps you see the differences in code structure.
- Only rawServer is functional if you run it as is.

Explanation

- Highlights how Node's built-in http module can be more verbose compared to a framework like Express.

Exercise 9: Simple API Logging with fs

Learning Objective

- Write basic logs to a file whenever an API endpoint is called.

```
// exercise9-logging.js
const http = require('http');
const fs = require('fs');
const server = http.createServer((req, res)
=> {
  if (req.url === '/api/log' && req.method
=== 'GET') {
    const logEntry = `Request on ${new
Date().toISOString()} - ${req.method}
${req.url}\n`;
    fs.appendFile('api.log', logEntry, (err)
=> {
```

```
      if (err) console.error('Failed to
log:', err);
    });
    res.writeHead(200, { 'Content-Type':
'application/json' });
    res.end(JSON.stringify({ status: 'logged'
}));
  } else {
    res.writeHead(404);
    res.end();
  }
});
server.listen(3010, () => {
  console.log('Logging API at
http://localhost:3010');
});
```

Outcome

- Each GET to /api/log appends a line to api.log
  with the current date/time.

Explanation

- Shows how to integrate Node's file system operations
  with an API for logging requests.

Exercise 10: Testing with Fetch in a Browser Console

Learning Objective

- Learn how to manually test a Node.js API using
  browser fetch (rather than Postman).

```
// exercise10-fetchDemo.js
```

```
// Not a server code, but instructions for
testing in your browser console:
/*
1. Run one of your previous servers, for
example exercise4-items.js on port 3004.
2. Open your browser's DevTools > Console,
and type:
   fetch('http://localhost:3004/api/items')
     .then(response => response.json())
     .then(data => console.log('Items:',
data))
     .catch(err => console.error('Fetch
error:', err));
3. For a POST request in the browser console
(if CORS allows):
   fetch('http://localhost:3004/api/items', {
     method: 'POST',
     headers: { 'Content-Type':
'application/json' },
     body: JSON.stringify({ item: 'Book' })
   })
     .then(response => response.json())
     .then(data => console.log('Created
item:', data))
     .catch(err => console.error('Fetch
error:', err));
*/
console.log("See the above comments for
instructions on how to test using fetch in
your browser console.");
```

Outcome

- Illustrates how to make GET/POST requests via
  fetch directly in the browser DevTools.

Explanation

167

- Practical demonstration of verifying your Node API without a separate client or Postman.

10 Multiple Choice Quiz Questions

Each question tests knowledge of creating and testing a simple API. Detailed answers follow each question.

1. **Which Node.js core module is primarily used to create a simple HTTP server that can serve API endpoints?**
   A. `fs`
   B. `path`
   C. `http`
   D. `crypto`
   Answer: C. `http`
   Explanation:
   - The `http` module is used to create and manage basic HTTP servers, including routes, request methods, and responses.
2. **What does REST in RESTful API stand for?**
   A. Rapid Event-based State Transfer
   B. Representational State Transfer
   C. Real-time Synchronous Transfer
   D. Resource Execution and Setup Translation
   Answer: B. Representational State Transfer
   Explanation:
   - REST is an architectural style focusing on stateless, resource-based interactions using standard HTTP methods.

3. **Which HTTP method is commonly used to retrieve data from a server?**
   A. GET
   B. POST
   C. PUT
   D. DELETE
   Answer: A. GET
   Explanation:
   - GET is the method for retrieving or reading resources from the server.
4. **Which HTTP method is typically used to create a new resource on the server?**
   A. GET
   B. POST
   C. PATCH
   D. CONNECT
   Answer: B. POST
   Explanation:
   - POST sends data to the server to create or add a new resource.
5. **In Node.js, how can you parse the request body for a JSON POST request without using external libraries like Express?**
   A. `request.json()`
   B. `request.body()`
   C. Using the `data` event on the request, concatenating chunks, and then `JSON.parse`
   D. Node.js automatically parses JSON by default
   Answer: C
   Explanation:
   - In raw Node, you must manually listen for `request.on('data')`, build the string, then `JSON.parse` it in `request.on('end')`.

6. **Which status code is typically returned when a resource is successfully created using a POST request?**
A. 200
B. 201
C. 202
D. 404
Answer: B. 201
Explanation:
   - HTTP 201 Created indicates a successful creation of a resource.

7. **If your Node.js API returns `res.writeHead(404)` and `res.end()`, what does this status code signify?**
A. The resource was created successfully
B. The requested resource was not found on the server
C. An internal server error occurred
D. You must authenticate to access this resource
Answer: B. The requested resource was not found on the server
Explanation:
   - `404 Not Found` is standard for resources or routes that do not exist.

8. **Which of the following is a valid way to test an API that runs on `http://localhost:3000/api/users`?**
A. Using a web browser directly if the endpoint responds with HTML
B. Using Postman or a similar tool to send GET/POST requests
C. Using the browser's DevTools Console and `fetch`
D. All of the above
Answer: D. All of the above
Explanation:
   - You can test an API using a browser (if it returns plain text or JSON), Postman, or `fetch` from DevTools console.

9. **What is an advantage of using Express or other frameworks over the native http module for APIs?**
A. They are always faster than native HTTP servers
B. They handle routing, parsing request bodies, and provide middleware out of the box
C. They replace the need for server-side logic entirely
D. They are included in the Node.js core modules
Answer: B
Explanation:
   o Frameworks like Express simplify tasks like routing, body parsing, error handling, etc. They are **not** faster by default; performance can vary.
10. **When designing a RESTful API, resources (like "users" or "items") are typically exposed as**:
A. One single endpoint for all operations
B. Different URLs representing each resource, e.g., `/api/users`, `/api/items`
C. Only one route for GET and one for POST, each handling all resources
D. Randomly generated URLs to access resources
Answer: B
Explanation:
   o REST recommends separate endpoints for different resources. For example: `/api/users`, `/api/users/:id`, `/api/items`.

Summary

By completing this chapter, you've learned:

1. **What an API is** and how it provides programmatic access to your Node.js application's data and functionality.
2. **Key RESTful principles**: resource-based URLs, stateless interactions, and the use of standard HTTP methods.

3. **Building basic GET/POST endpoints** using Node's native `http` module—creating a minimal but functional JSON-based API.
4. **Testing your API** with Postman, browser fetch, or other HTTP clients.

The **10 coding exercises** have given you hands-on experience adding, retrieving, filtering, validating, and logging data via your API, while the **multiple-choice questions** reinforce the fundamentals of REST and Node.js HTTP handling. With these skills, you can build more complex endpoints, integrate databases, and scale your API to production-ready levels.

Chapter 10. Next Steps and Learning Resources

You've learned the fundamentals of Node.js: setting up your environment, building basic HTTP servers, understanding asynchronous programming, and even creating simple APIs. **Where do you go from here?** In this chapter, we'll suggest ways to expand your Node.js skill set—focusing on popular libraries and frameworks like **Express.js**, exploring databases like **MongoDB**, and providing practice project ideas. We'll also point you to resources for further study so you can continue your journey as a Node.js developer.

1. Expanding Your Knowledge

1.1. Learn About Express.js

While you can build servers with Node's native `http` module, **Express.js** is a minimal but powerful framework that simplifies:

- **Routing**: Define multiple endpoints with clean, concise syntax.

- **Middleware**: Use or create reusable functions for tasks like parsing JSON, handling authentication, or logging.
- **Error Handling**: Centralize how your application deals with exceptions.

Why Express.js?

- **Popularity**: It's one of the most widely used Node.js frameworks.
- **Rich Ecosystem**: Thousands of middleware packages for tasks like security, sessions, templating, etc.
- **Simplicity**: Quick to set up a basic server and scale to more complex apps.

1.2. Explore Working with Databases (MongoDB)

Once your Node.js apps need persistent data, you'll likely connect to a database. **MongoDB** is a popular, beginner-friendly choice due to:

- **Document-Oriented**: Stores data in JSON-like documents instead of strict tables.
- **Flexible Schema**: Easy to evolve your data structure.
- **Rich Ecosystem**: Tools like **Mongoose** simplify working with MongoDB in Node.js.

Example flow for using MongoDB:

1. **Install MongoDB** or use a cloud service like MongoDB Atlas.
2. **Use a driver** (like the official `mongodb` package) or an **ODM** (Object Data Modeling) library like **Mongoose**.
3. **Connect** to MongoDB from your Node.js app and define how data is stored, retrieved, and updated.

2. Practice Projects for Beginners

2.1. Build a Basic To-Do List App

- **Objective**: Create an Express-based server that allows users to create, read, update, and delete tasks.
- **Features**:
  - **GET /todos**: Retrieves all tasks.
  - **POST /todos**: Creates a new task.
  - **PUT /todos/:id**: Updates an existing task.
  - **DELETE /todos/:id**: Removes a task.
- **Storage**: Start with in-memory arrays, then upgrade to a database (e.g., MongoDB).

2.2. Create a Random Joke Generator

- **Objective**: Serve random jokes (or quotes) via an API endpoint.
- **Features**:
  - **GET /jokes/random**: Returns one random joke from a predefined list.
  - (Optional) **POST /jokes**: Add new jokes to your data store.
- **Enhanced Variation**: Add categories or tags, handle GET requests for jokes by category.

3. Recommended Resources

1. **Official Node.js Documentation**:
   - https://nodejs.org/en/docs/
   - Updated with each Node.js release, covering APIs and best practices.
2. **Express.js Documentation**:
   - https://expressjs.com/
   - Detailed guides and examples for routing, middleware, error handling, etc.

3. **MongoDB Documentation**:
    - https://www.mongodb.com/docs/
    - Clear tutorials on database setup, CRUD operations, and indexes.
4. **Beginner-Friendly Tutorials and Courses**:
    - Free code-based tutorials on sites like **Codecademy, FreeCodeCamp**, or **MDN Web Docs**.
    - Online video platforms (e.g., YouTube, Udemy) offering beginner Node.js walkthroughs.

10 Coding Exercises

Below are ten exercises designed to help you transition from basic Node.js concepts to building and structuring more advanced applications. Each includes:

1. **Learning Objective**
2. **Full Code** (where applicable)
3. **Outcome**
4. **Explanation**

Feel free to adapt or expand them for deeper learning.

Exercise 1: Your First Express.js Server

Learning Objective: Install and use Express.js to create a basic server responding with "Hello Express!".

Install Express in a new project:

```
npm init -y
npm install express
```

Create exercise1-express.js:

```
// exercise1-express.js
const express = require('express');
```

```
const app = express();
app.get('/', (req, res) => {
  res.send('Hello Express!');
});
app.listen(4000, () => {
  console.log('Express server listening on
http://localhost:4000');
});
```
Run:

```
node exercise1-express.js
```

1. **Outcome:**
   o Visit `http://localhost:4000` in your
     browser to see "Hello Express!".

Explanation:

- Demonstrates how Express handles routing with
  `app.get`.
- `app.listen` starts the server on port 4000.

Exercise 2: Express JSON Endpoint

Learning Objective: Respond with JSON data instead of
plain text.

```
// exercise2-express-json.js
const express = require('express');
const app = express();
app.get('/api/info', (req, res) => {
  const info = {
    message: 'Express with JSON response',
    timestamp: new Date().toISOString()
  };
  res.json(info);
```

```
});
app.listen(4001, () => {
  console.log('Server running at
http://localhost:4001');
});
```

1. **Run** node exercise2-express-json.js.
2. **Outcome**:
   - GET http://localhost:4001/api/info
     returns JSON like { "message": "...",
     "timestamp": "..." }.

Explanation:

- res.json() automatically sets the Content-Type to
  application/json.

Exercise 3: Basic Mongoose Connection (MongoDB)

Learning Objective: Learn how to install **mongoose** and connect to a MongoDB database.

Install mongoose:

```
npm install mongoose
```
Create exercise3-mongoose.js:

```
// exercise3-mongoose.js
const mongoose = require('mongoose');
// Replace with your actual MongoDB URI or
local connection string
const uri =
'mongodb://127.0.0.1:27017/testdb';
mongoose
  .connect(uri)
```

```
.then(() => {
  console.log('Connected to MongoDB
successfully!');
  process.exit(0); // Exit after successful
connection test
})
.catch((err) => {
  console.error('Connection error:', err);
});
```
Run:

```
node exercise3-mongoose.js
```

1. **Outcome**:
    o If `testdb` exists (or is created automatically),
      logs "Connected to MongoDB successfully!".

Explanation:

- Illustrates how to connect to a local MongoDB instance
  or a remote cluster.
- In real apps, you'd keep the connection open to run
  queries.

Exercise 4: Defining a Mongoose Model

Learning Objective: Create a **User** model and insert a
document into MongoDB.

```
// exercise4-userModel.js
const mongoose = require('mongoose');
const uri =
'mongodb://127.0.0.1:27017/testdb';
const userSchema = new mongoose.Schema({
  name: String,
  email: String,
  age: Number
```

```javascript
});
const User = mongoose.model('User',
userSchema);
mongoose
  .connect(uri)
  .then(async () => {
    console.log('MongoDB connected.');
    // Create a new user
    const newUser = new User({
      name: 'Alice',
      email: 'alice@example.com',
      age: 25
    });
    const savedUser = await newUser.save();
    console.log('User saved:', savedUser);
    process.exit(0); // Exit script
  })
  .catch((err) => {
    console.error('Connection error:', err);
  });
```

1. **Outcome**:
   - Creates a document in `testdb.users`
     collection, logs the saved user.

Explanation:

- `mongoose.Schema` defines structure of the
  documents.
- `User` is a model representing that collection in
  MongoDB.

Exercise 5: Building a Simple To-Do API with Express + Mongoose

Learning Objective: Combine Express and MongoDB to perform basic CRUD operations on a to-do collection.

```
// exercise5-todoApi.js
const express = require('express');
const mongoose = require('mongoose');
mongoose.connect('mongodb://127.0.0.1:27017/t
ododb').catch(console.error);
const todoSchema = new mongoose.Schema({
  text: String,
  completed: { type: Boolean, default: false
}
});
const Todo = mongoose.model('Todo',
todoSchema);
const app = express();
app.use(express.json());
// GET all todos
app.get('/api/todos', async (req, res) => {
  const todos = await Todo.find({});
  res.json(todos);
});
// POST new todo
app.post('/api/todos', async (req, res) => {
  const newTodo = new Todo(req.body);
  const saved = await newTodo.save();
  res.status(201).json(saved);
});
// Mark complete
app.patch('/api/todos/:id', async (req, res)
=> {
  const { id } = req.params;
```

```
  const updated = await
Todo.findByIdAndUpdate(id, req.body, { new:
true });
  if (!updated) {
    return res.status(404).json({ error:
'Todo not found' });
  }
  res.json(updated);
});
app.listen(4002, () => {
  console.log('To-Do API on
http://localhost:4002');
});
```

1. **Outcome**:
   - GET /api/todos => all todos,
   - POST /api/todos => create a new one,
   - PATCH /api/todos/:id => partial updates (like completing a task).

Explanation:

- Demonstrates real-world usage: an Express server, JSON body parsing, Mongoose for data persistence, and multiple routes.

Exercise 6: Random Joke Generator with Express

Learning Objective: Create an endpoint returning a random item from an array of jokes.

```
// exercise6-jokeApi.js
const express = require('express');
const app = express();
const jokes = [
```

```
  "Why don't programmers like nature? It has
too many bugs.",
  "How many programmers does it take to
change a light bulb? None, it's a hardware
problem.",
  "Programmer: A machine that turns coffee
into code."
];
app.get('/api/jokes/random', (req, res) => {
  const randomIndex =
Math.floor(Math.random() * jokes.length);
  res.json({ joke: jokes[randomIndex] });
});
app.listen(4003, () => {
  console.log('Joke API running at
http://localhost:4003');
});
```

1. **Outcome**:
   o GET `/api/jokes/random` returns `{ "joke": "some random joke" }`.

Explanation:

- Showcases a straightforward approach to randomizing output.

Exercise 7: Implementing Middleware in Express

Learning Objective: Understand how to create a simple middleware that logs incoming request methods and paths.

```
// exercise7-middleware.js
const express = require('express');
const app = express();
```

182

```javascript
// Custom logger middleware
app.use((req, res, next) => {
  console.log(`Incoming request:
${req.method} ${req.url}`);
  next(); // proceed to next middleware or
route
});
app.get('/', (req, res) => {
  res.send('Middleware Example: check your
console for logs.');
});
app.listen(4004, () => {
  console.log('Middleware server at
http://localhost:4004');
});
```

1. **Outcome**:
    o Every request logs `Incoming request:`
      `<METHOD> <URL>` in the console.

Explanation:

- Demonstrates the concept of Express middleware for logging or other cross-cutting concerns.

Exercise 8: Error Handling Middleware in Express

Learning Objective: Show how to handle errors gracefully and return consistent JSON messages.

```javascript
// exercise8-errorMiddleware.js
const express = require('express');
const app = express();
// JSON parse error simulation
app.get('/throw-error', (req, res, next) => {
```

```
  try {
    JSON.parse('invalidJSON');
  } catch (err) {
    next(err); // pass error to error-
handling middleware
  }
});
app.use((err, req, res, next) => {
  console.error('Error middleware caught:',
err.message);
  res.status(500).json({ error: 'Internal
Server Error' });
});
app.listen(4005, () => {
  console.log('Error handling server at
http://localhost:4005');
});
```

1. **Outcome**:
   - Visiting `/throw-error` triggers a JSON parse error, caught by the error middleware.
   - Returns `{ "error": "Internal Server Error" }` with a 500 status.

Explanation:

- In Express, error-handling middleware has four parameters: `(err, req, res, next)`.

Exercise 9: Basic Unit Test Setup (Mocha & Chai)

Learning Objective: Encourage testing next steps. Show how to test a simple function using Mocha & Chai (though not an Express route itself).

Install dev dependencies:

```
npm install --save-dev mocha chai
```
Create exercise9-test.js:

```
// exercise9-test.js
const { expect } = require('chai');
function add(a, b) {
  return a + b;
}
describe('add function tests', () => {
  it('should return the correct sum', () => {
    expect(add(2, 3)).to.equal(5);
  });
  it('should handle negative numbers', () =>
{
    expect(add(-2, 4)).to.equal(2);
  });
});
```
Update package.json script:

```
{
  "scripts": {
    "test": "mocha"
  }
}
```

1. **Run** npm test.

Outcome:

- Mocha runs the tests, logs passing results.

Explanation:

- Demonstrates how to set up a simple test environment.

- Next step: test your Express routes or DB queries with this approach.

Exercise 10: Searching External APIs with Node Fetch (or axios)

Learning Objective: Expand on your Node knowledge by calling external APIs.

```
// exercise10-fetchApi.js
// Using Node's built-in "fetch" from node >=
18 or installing 'node-fetch' in older
versions
// For older Node versions: npm install node-
fetch@2
const fetch = (...args) =>
  import('node-fetch').then(({ default: fetch
}) => fetch(...args)); // for Node < 18
snippet, if needed
(async () => {
  try {
    const response = await
fetch('https://api.chucknorris.io/jokes/rando
m');
    const json = await response.json();
    console.log('Random Chuck Norris Joke:',
json.value);
  } catch (error) {
    console.error('Fetch error:', error);
  }
})();
```

1. **Outcome**:
   o Logs a random Chuck Norris joke from the external API.

Explanation:

- Demonstrates how Node can consume external APIs, just like front-end code.
- If using Node 18 or higher, `global.fetch` is available by default (experimental). For older versions, you can use `node-fetch`.

10 Multiple Choice Quiz Questions

Below are ten questions about next steps with Node.js, databases, frameworks, and recommended learning paths. Each answer includes a detailed explanation.

1. **Which of the following is the main reason developers use Express.js instead of Node's native `http` module?**
   A. Express is more secure out of the box
   B. Express code always runs faster
   C. Express provides a simpler API for routing, middleware, and error handling
   D. Express is included in the Node core
   Answer: C. Express provides a simpler API for routing, middleware, and error handling
   Explanation:
   - Express is not inherently more secure or faster by default, but it offers a cleaner development workflow for building web applications.

2. **What is MongoDB best known for?**
   A. Being a relational database with strict schemas
   B. Storing data as documents in a JSON-like format
   C. Requiring complex SQL queries
   D. Only working on Windows servers
   Answer: B. Storing data as documents in a JSON-like format
   Explanation:
   - MongoDB is a NoSQL database, using flexible, document-oriented storage.

3. **Which Express middleware is commonly used to parse JSON request bodies in modern Express applications?**
A. `bodyParser.json()` (or `app.use(express.json())`)
B. `urlencoded-parser`
C. `cookie-session`
D. No middleware is required for JSON
Answer: **A. `bodyParser.json()`** or using **`express.json()`** directly
Explanation:
   - In older Express versions, `body-parser` was the go-to. Since Express 4.16+, `express.json()` is built-in.
4. **If you want to handle advanced data relationships in Node.js, which library is popular for working with MongoDB?**
A. `sqlite`
B. `mongoose`
C. `pg`
D. `redis`
Answer: **B. `mongoose`**
Explanation:
   - `mongoose` is an ODM (Object Data Modeling) library that helps manage schemas and relationships in MongoDB.
5. **When building a to-do list app, which HTTP method is typically used to create a new task?**
A. GET
B. POST
C. PUT
D. DELETE
Answer: **B. POST**
Explanation:
   - POST is used to add/create new resources on the server side.

6. **Which statement about building a random joke generator in Node.js is true?**
A. You must store jokes in a database for it to work
B. You can store jokes in an array or an external file, then serve them randomly
C. Node.js cannot handle random logic
D. Express is mandatory for serving random data
Answer: B. You can store jokes in an array or an external file, then serve them randomly
Explanation:
   - A random joke endpoint can be built with or without Express, and data storage can be as simple as an array or as complex as a database.
7. **Which resource is not recommended for Node.js beginners?**
A. Official Node.js docs
B. Random unverified code from unknown sources without explanation
C. FreeCodeCamp tutorials
D. Express.js official documentation
Answer: B. Random unverified code from unknown sources without explanation
Explanation:
   - All the others (official docs, recognized tutorials) are safe, thorough resources for learning best practices.
8. **In a basic Express server, if you define** `app.get('/users', handler)`, **what happens if a request is made to POST /users?**
A. It will use the same handler as GET
B. It will return a 405 Method Not Allowed by default
C. It will result in a 404 Not Found if no other route is defined
D. The request automatically becomes a GET request
Answer: C. It will result in a 404 Not Found if no other route is defined
Explanation:

- An Express route is method-specific. If only GET is defined, a POST request to the same path is unmatched, resulting in 404 unless otherwise handled.

9. **What is an advantage of writing tests for your Node.js code using frameworks like Mocha or Jest?**
   A. It slows down development intentionally
   B. Ensures that changes don't unintentionally break existing functionality
   C. It only helps when writing database logic
   D. Testing is too advanced for beginners
   Answer: B. Ensures that changes don't unintentionally break existing functionality
   Explanation:
   - Automated testing fosters confidence in your codebase, preventing regressions.

10. **Which is a practical next step after learning Node.js basics?**
    A. Abandon Node.js and switch to a different language
    B. Use Node.js only for static HTML files
    C. Learn a framework like Express, integrate a database, and build bigger projects
    D. Avoid building real applications to reduce complexity
    Answer: C. Learn a framework like Express, integrate a database, and build bigger projects
    Explanation:
    - Mastering Node.js best comes from tackling real-world tasks: routing, databases, security, testing, etc.

Wrap-Up

You've now reached a pivotal stage in your Node.js learning journey. While you've covered fundamental concepts, there's much more you can explore:

- **Express.js** and other frameworks for cleaner, more organized server code.
- **MongoDB** (and other databases) for persistent data.
- **Testing tools** (Mocha, Jest) to ensure code reliability.
- **Practice Projects** (to-do apps, random joke generators) to solidify your skills.

By following these steps and leveraging recommended resources such as official documentation, beginner-friendly tutorials, and coding communities, you'll continue to grow as a Node.js developer. Building real applications—complete with routing, databases, error handling, and tests—will ensure you're ready for more advanced topics, from scaling your Node.js apps in production to exploring specialized libraries for websockets, security, or microservices. Keep coding, keep experimenting, and enjoy your journey into the broader Node.js ecosystem!

Quiz Questions

Section 1: Introduction to Node.js

1. **Which statement best describes Node.js?**
   A. A JavaScript front-end framework for building mobile apps
   B. A JavaScript runtime environment built on Chrome's V8 engine
   C. A relational database for storing JSON documents
   D. A tool that only runs JavaScript in the browser
   Correct Answer: B. A JavaScript runtime environment built on Chrome's V8 engine
   Explanation:
   Node.js is a **server-side runtime** that lets you execute JavaScript outside the browser. It leverages Google's V8 engine for performance and JIT compilation.

2. **Before Node.js, JavaScript was primarily used for which purpose?**
A. Operating System development
B. Server-side applications
C. Database management scripts
D. Client-side web development in browsers
Correct Answer: D. Client-side web development in browsers
Explanation:
Traditionally, JavaScript was mostly utilized in the browser to manipulate HTML and CSS (the DOM). Node.js changed that by bringing JavaScript to the server side.

3. **What is the primary advantage of Node.js's non-blocking I/O model?**
A. It allows Node.js to run multiple threads by default
B. It enables Node.js to handle multiple concurrent requests without blocking
C. It blocks all file system and network operations until they complete
D. It converts JavaScript to machine code for faster execution
Correct Answer: B. It enables Node.js to handle multiple concurrent requests without blocking
Explanation:
Node.js uses an event-driven, non-blocking I/O model to process many requests in a single thread. While one operation is waiting (e.g., for file I/O), Node.js can handle other tasks.

4. **Which feature contributed to Node.js's popularity for server-side development?**
   A. Separation of JavaScript from the V8 engine
   B. Built-in multi-threading with automatic load balancing
   C. A massive package ecosystem through npm
   D. Mandatory use of TypeScript
   Correct Answer: C. A massive package ecosystem through npm
   Explanation:
   The npm registry is one of the largest repositories of open-source libraries, enabling rapid development with countless modules for different use cases.
5. **Who originally created Node.js in 2009?**
   A. Tim Berners-Lee
   B. Ryan Dahl
   C. Brendan Eich
   D. Guido van Rossum
   Correct Answer: B. Ryan Dahl
   Explanation:
   Ryan Dahl created Node.js, motivated by the need to improve how servers handle many simultaneous network connections.

6. **Which statement about Node.js's event-driven architecture is true?**

A. Node.js spawns a new thread for each incoming request

B. Node.js blocks all other tasks while a file is reading from disk

C. Node.js uses an event loop to manage callbacks and schedule tasks

D. Node.js requires a separate event loop for each I/O operation

Correct Answer: C. Node.js uses an event loop to manage callbacks and schedule tasks

Explanation:

The single-threaded event loop is central to Node.js. It handles events and callbacks without creating multiple threads for each connection.

7. **What is npm in the Node.js ecosystem?**

A. A built-in module for reading files

B. A package manager that installs and manages dependencies

C. A protocol for transferring data between client and server

D. A database engine included with Node.js by default

Correct Answer: B. A package manager that installs and manages dependencies

Explanation:

The Node Package Manager (npm) is automatically installed with Node.js and is used to download, install, and maintain third-party packages.

8. **Which of the following best describes the single-threaded nature of Node.js?**
A. Node.js cannot perform asynchronous operations
B. Node.js uses one thread for the main event loop, but can delegate tasks to background workers
C. Node.js creates a thread pool with thousands of threads by default
D. Node.js only runs on single-core processors
Correct Answer: B. Node.js uses one thread for the main event loop, but can delegate tasks to background workers
Explanation:
Node.js manages concurrency in a single-threaded event loop, but non-blocking tasks like file/network I/O are offloaded to the Node.js worker pool (libuv) behind the scenes.

9. **Which is not an advantage of Node.js's approach to server-side programming?**
A. Excellent for real-time web applications
B. Offers a large ecosystem of open-source packages
C. Automatically scales CPU-bound tasks across all processor cores
D. Makes it easy to handle many concurrent network requests
Correct Answer: C. Automatically scales CPU-bound tasks across all processor cores
Explanation:
Node.js doesn't automatically split CPU-intensive tasks across multiple cores. For that, you'd typically use the cluster module or worker threads.

10. **Which company is not commonly associated with using Node.js in production?**
A. Netflix
B. NASA
C. LinkedIn
D. MySQL (as a database engine)
Correct Answer: D. MySQL (as a database engine)
Explanation:
MySQL is a relational database engine, not a Node.js-based application. Netflix, NASA, and LinkedIn have famously adopted Node.js for various parts of their tech stack.

Section 2: Setting Up Node.js

1. **Which command verifies your Node.js version after installation?**
A. `node --verify`
B. `node -v`
C. `npm -nodeVersion`
D. `npm start`
Correct Answer: B. `node -v`
Explanation:
`node -v` prints the version of Node.js installed on your system. `npm -v` prints the npm version.

2. **What does `npm init -y` do?**
A. Uninstalls all packages in `node_modules`
B. Installs Node.js globally
C. Creates a default `package.json` file with all prompts skipped
D. Performs a dry run of installing dependencies
Correct Answer: C. Creates a default `package.json` file with all prompts skipped
Explanation:
The `-y` flag answers "yes" to all interactive prompts, generating a `package.json` with default values.

3. **Which directory typically holds locally installed npm packages?**
   A. `node_modules`
   B. `packages`
   C. `src`
   D. `lib`
   Correct Answer: A. `node_modules`
   Explanation:
   When you run `npm install <package>`, the package is placed into the `node_modules` folder in your project directory.

4. **What is a common reason to install Node.js via a version manager like nvm?**
   A. To have multiple Node.js versions installed and switch between them easily
   B. To automatically compile TypeScript to JavaScript
   C. To keep all Node.js packages up to date with a single command
   D. To integrate directly with MySQL databases
   Correct Answer: A. To have multiple Node.js versions installed and switch between them easily
   Explanation:
   A Node version manager (like nvm) helps developers test or run different Node.js versions without conflicts.

5. **Which file includes metadata about your Node.js project, like its name, version, and dependencies?**
   A. `package.json`
   B. `node.json`
   C. `init.js`
   D. `package-lock.json`
   Correct Answer: A. `package.json`
   Explanation:
   `package.json` stores your project's metadata, scripts, and a list of dependencies. It's created via `npm init`.

6. **What does `npm install --save-dev nodemon` do?**

   A. Installs nodemon globally for all projects on your system

   B. Installs nodemon as a regular dependency for production use

   C. Installs nodemon as a dev dependency, listed under devDependencies in `package.json`

   D. Removes nodemon from your local project

   Correct Answer: C. Installs nodemon as a dev dependency, listed under devDependencies in `package.json`

   Explanation:

   The `--save-dev` (or `-D`) flag stores the package in devDependencies, indicating it's primarily for development tools.

7. **If you see a `package-lock.json` file, what does it indicate?**

   A. It locks the operating system version used to run Node.js

   B. It locks exact versions of dependencies to ensure consistent installs

   C. It is a backup copy of `package.json`

   D. It's required only in older Node.js versions

   Correct Answer: B. It locks exact versions of dependencies to ensure consistent installs

   Explanation:

   `package-lock.json` is generated automatically, tracking the exact dependency tree (including sub-dependencies) for reproducible builds.

8. **Which command would you use to install a package like `http-server` globally?**
   A. `npm install http-server`
   B. `npm install --global http-server`
   C. `npm local --http-server`
   D. `node install -g http-server`
   Correct Answer: B. `npm install --global http-server`
   Explanation:
   The `-g` or `--global` flag installs the package system-wide, making `http-server` available as a command in your terminal from any location.
9. **Why might a developer prefer local package installation over global installation?**
   A. So the package is always available from the command line for any project
   B. To avoid adding dependencies to `package.json`
   C. To ensure consistent versions across different projects and environments
   D. Because local packages cannot be published to npm
   Correct Answer: C. To ensure consistent versions across different projects and environments
   Explanation:
   Local installations tie the dependency version to each project. This prevents version conflicts between multiple projects on the same machine.

10. Which command automatically creates default answers for fields like **name**, **version**, and **description** in **package.json**?
    A. npm init
    B. npm init -y
    C. npm install
    D. npm run default
    Correct Answer: B. npm init -y
    Explanation:
    As mentioned, npm init -y automatically initializes package.json without asking the interactive setup questions, using defaults for each field.

Section 3: Writing Your First Node.js Program

1. Which command do you use to execute a JavaScript file named **app.js** in Node.js?
    A. npm app.js
    B. node app.js
    C. npm start app.js
    D. run app.js
    Correct Answer: B. node app.js
    Explanation:
    node <filename> is the standard approach to run a Node.js script.

2. **If you type node without a filename in your terminal, what environment are you starting?**
A. The npm environment
B. The Node.js REPL (Read-Eval-Print Loop)
C. A global debugging mode
D. A Node server with port 3000
Correct Answer: B. The Node.js REPL (Read-Eval-Print Loop)
Explanation:
Running node by itself launches an interactive shell for evaluating JavaScript expressions in real time.

3. **Which global function is used in Node.js to print output to the console?**
A. `console.log()`
B. `alert()`
C. `prompt()`
D. `window.log()`
Correct Answer: A. `console.log()`
Explanation:
`console.log()` is the canonical way to display messages or variables in Node.js (and in browsers' developer consoles).

4. **What happens if you use `console.log("Hello");` in the Node.js REPL?**
A. It displays an alert in the browser window
B. It prints "Hello" to the terminal console
C. It writes "Hello" to `package.json`
D. It does nothing
Correct Answer: B. It prints "Hello" to the terminal console
Explanation:
The Node.js REPL and environment output logs to the terminal or command prompt window.

5. **Which statement about the Node.js REPL is correct?**
   A. It blocks system operations while waiting for user input
   B. It only accepts synchronous code
   C. It allows you to type JavaScript commands and immediately see results
   D. It must be installed separately from Node.js
   Correct Answer: C. It allows you to type JavaScript commands and immediately see results
   Explanation:
   The REPL is an interactive environment for quick experimentation and debugging. No separate install is needed.

6. **If your file `hello.js` contains `console.log("Hello World");`, how do you run it?**
   A. `node run hello.js`
   B. `npm hello.js`
   C. `node hello.js`
   D. `npm start hello.js`
   Correct Answer: C. `node hello.js`
   Explanation:
   This is the standard command to run a Node.js script named `hello.js`.

7. **How do you exit the Node.js REPL?**
   A. Type `.exit` or press `Ctrl + C` twice
   B. Type `Ctrl + Z`
   C. Type `exit();`
   D. You cannot exit without closing the terminal
   Correct Answer: A. Type `.exit` or press `Ctrl + C` twice
   Explanation:
   These are the two standard ways to exit the Node.js REPL. Pressing `Ctrl + C` once interrupts the current command, pressing it twice exits.

8. If you add `console.log("End of file");` after an asynchronous operation, what will happen in Node.js?

   A. The async result is always printed before "End of file"

   B. "End of file" may appear first if the async operation hasn't completed yet

   C. The console log will block everything until the async operation ends

   D. Node.js does not allow asynchronous operations

   Correct Answer: B. "End of file" may appear first if the async operation hasn't completed yet

   Explanation:

   Since Node.js is non-blocking, your async function may complete after subsequent synchronous logs.

9. **What is the purpose of using the Node.js REPL for learning or testing?**

   A. To run production servers at scale

   B. To debug code within a complex framework automatically

   C. To quickly test small JavaScript snippets without creating a file

   D. To compile JavaScript to binary executables

   Correct Answer: C. To quickly test small JavaScript snippets without creating a file

   Explanation:

   The REPL is excellent for quick code experiments, verifying logic, or debugging variables without a full script.

10. **Which expression will the Node.js REPL show as the result if you type 2 + 2 and press Enter?**
    A. 2 + 2
    B. undefined
    C. 4
    D. A syntax error
    Correct Answer: C. 4
    Explanation:
    The REPL evaluates the input and shows the resulting value. For 2 + 2, that's 4.

Section 4: Node.js Core Modules

1. **Which of the following is not a core module in Node.js?**
   A. fs
   B. http
   C. path
   D. axios
   Correct Answer: D. axios
   Explanation:
   axios is a third-party HTTP client library. Modules like fs, http, path, and os are core Node.js modules.

2. **Which core module in Node.js provides methods for reading and writing files?**
   A. events
   B. fs
   C. crypto
   D. url
   Correct Answer: B. fs
   Explanation:
   The **File System** (fs) module includes methods like readFile, writeFile, appendFile, etc.

3. Which method in the **path** module normalizes a file
   path, resolving .. and . segments?
   A. `path.join()`
   B. `path.normalize()`
   C. `path.clean()`
   D. `path.parse()`
   Correct Answer: **B. `path.normalize()`**
   Explanation:
   `path.normalize()` corrects path string irregularities
   like redundant slashes or ./.. references.
4. Which Node.js core module helps create basic HTTP
   servers?
   A. `http`
   B. `fs`
   C. `stream`
   D. `querystring`
   Correct Answer: **A. `http`**
   Explanation:
   The `http` module is fundamental for spinning up a
   web server and handling requests/responses in
   Node.js.
5. If you want to retrieve your system's CPU and
   memory information, which core module would you
   use?
   A. `os`
   B. `crypto`
   C. `zlib`
   D. `buffer`
   Correct Answer: **A. `os`**
   Explanation:
   `os` has methods like `os.cpus()`, `os.totalmem()`,
   and `os.freemem()` for system information.

6. **Which method do you call on an HTTP server instance to start listening for connections?**
A. `server.bind()`
B. `server.execute()`
C. `server.listen()`
D. `server.run()`
Correct Answer: C. `server.listen()`
Explanation:
After `http.createServer(...)`, you call `server.listen(port, callback)` to begin accepting requests.

7. **What is the purpose of the `events` module in Node.js?**
A. Creating a new process for each event
B. Managing custom event emission and handling in an event-driven architecture
C. Handling file system changes automatically
D. Loading environment variables from a .env file
Correct Answer: B. Managing custom event emission and handling in an event-driven architecture
Explanation:
The `events` module allows you to create an `EventEmitter` instance, registering listeners and emitting events in your application logic.

8. **Which Node.js core module is frequently used to perform cryptographic functions like hashing?**
A. `crypto`
B. `buffer`
C. `dns`
D. `zlib`
Correct Answer: A. `crypto`
Explanation:
The `crypto` module provides cryptographic functionalities such as hashing and generating secure random values.

9. **Which method from the fs module appends data to a file without overwriting it?**
   A. `fs.writeFile()`
   B. `fs.appendFile()`
   C. `fs.readFile()`
   D. `fs.copyFile()`
   Correct Answer: **B. `fs.appendFile()`**
   Explanation:
   `appendFile` places new data at the end of an existing file, creating the file if it doesn't exist.
10. **Which best describes how Node.js core modules are imported in your script?**
    A. `const module = require('module');`
    B. `import module from 'module';` only
    C. Using npm to install them first
    D. Node.js does not have built-in modules
    Correct Answer: **A. `const module = require('module');`**
    Explanation:
    Node.js core modules are available by default and are commonly imported using the `require` function (CommonJS). Modern Node can also use ES modules with `import`, given the correct configuration.

Section 5: Building a Simple HTTP Server

1. **Which module is primarily used to create an HTTP server in Node.js?**
   A. `path`
   B. `http`
   C. `events`
   D. `child_process`
   Correct Answer: **B. `http`**
   Explanation:
   The `http` module provides `createServer()` to handle HTTP requests and responses.

2. **In a basic Node.js HTTP server, which object represents the incoming request details?**
   A. `req`
   B. `res`
   C. `server`
   D. `requestInfo`
   Correct Answer: A. `req`
   Explanation:
   Inside `http.createServer((req, res) => {...})`, `req` is the incoming request object, containing URL, method, headers, etc.

3. **What does `res.writeHead(200, {'Content-Type': 'text/plain'})` typically signify in a Node.js server?**
   A. It sets a 200 status code and content type for a plain text response
   B. It writes the HTTP request to console
   C. It blocks further operations until the request completes
   D. It sets a 404 status by default
   Correct Answer: A. It sets a 200 status code and content type for a plain text response
   Explanation:
   `res.writeHead()` defines the HTTP status code and headers. 200 means success, `text/plain` indicates plain text data.

4. **Which method finishes sending the response in a Node.js HTTP server?**
   A. `res.final()`
   B. `res.close()`
   C. `res.end()`
   D. `res.exit()`
   Correct Answer: C. `res.end()`
   Explanation:
   `res.end()` signals the end of the response, sending the content to the client. No more data can be written after calling `res.end()`.

5. **What is the typical usage of**
   `server.listen(3000)`?
   A. Binds the server to port 80
   B. Starts listening on port 3000 for HTTP requests
   C. Binds all server methods to the console
   D. Automatically logs all requests
   Correct Answer: B. Starts listening on port 3000 for HTTP requests
   Explanation:
   Port 3000 is commonly used in Node.js examples. `listen` means the server will accept requests on that port.

6. **Which status code is commonly sent to indicate a "Not Found" error when no route matches?**
   A. 200
   B. 201
   C. 400
   D. 404
   Correct Answer: D. 404
   Explanation:
   `404 Not Found` is the standard HTTP status code for a resource/URL that doesn't exist on the server.

7. **How can you handle different endpoints in a basic Node.js HTTP server without any framework?**
   A. By reading `req.url` and `req.method` and using if-else or switch logic
   B. By automatically mapping URLs to file names
   C. By installing the `fs` module
   D. By creating multiple servers
   Correct Answer: A. By reading `req.url` and `req.method` and using if-else or switch logic
   Explanation:
   In a raw `http` server, you typically check `req.url` and `req.method` to decide how to respond.

8. **What happens if `res.end()` is never called in a Node.js HTTP server?**
   A. The server automatically closes the response after 1 second
   B. The request remains open and the client hangs waiting for data
   C. A default "Hello World" message is sent automatically
   D. Node.js throws a syntax error
   Correct Answer: B. The request remains open and the client hangs waiting for data
   Explanation:
   Without calling `res.end()`, you never finalize the response. The connection may stay open until the server or client times out.

9. **Which header is important to set when returning JSON data from a Node.js server?**
   A. `Content-Type: text/plain`
   B. `Content-Type: application/json`
   C. `Accept: application/json`
   D. `X-JSON: true`
   Correct Answer: B. `Content-Type: application/json`
   Explanation:
   This tells clients (browsers, fetch libraries, etc.) to interpret the response as JSON.

10. **What is the simplest way to verify a basic Node.js server running on port 3000 is functioning?**
A. You must always use Postman or cURL
B. Type `http://localhost:3000` into a web browser address bar
C. Node.js servers only accept cURL requests
D. Wait for an email confirmation from the server
Correct Answer: B. Type `http://localhost:3000` into a web browser address bar
Explanation:
Browsers can connect to `localhost` for local development. If your server returns any content or message, you'll see it there.

Section 6: Working with the File System

1. **Which Node.js module do you use to interact with the file system (reading, writing files)?**
A. `path`
B. `fs`
C. `http`
D. `cluster`
Correct Answer: B. `fs`
Explanation:
`fs` stands for File System, containing methods like `readFile`, `writeFile`, etc.
2. **Which method reads a file asynchronously, then invokes a callback when done?**
A. `fs.readFileSync()`
B. `fs.readFile()`
C. `fs.read()`
D. `fs.loadFile()`
Correct Answer: B. `fs.readFile()`
Explanation:
`readFileSync` is synchronous, blocking the process. `fs.readFile()` is asynchronous, taking a callback.

211

3. **What is the main difference between fs.readFile() and fs.readFileSync()?**
   A. fs.readFile() can only read text files, while fs.readFileSync() reads binary files
   B. fs.readFile() is synchronous, fs.readFileSync() is asynchronous
   C. fs.readFile() is asynchronous, fs.readFileSync() is synchronous
   D. Both are asynchronous, but fs.readFileSync() reads from a remote server
   Correct Answer: C. fs.readFile() is asynchronous, fs.readFileSync() is synchronous
   Explanation:
   The "Sync" variants block the main thread until the operation completes, while the asynchronous versions rely on callbacks or promises.

4. **Which method in the fs module overwrites or creates a new file with the given content?**
   A. fs.appendFile()
   B. fs.writeFile()
   C. fs.rename()
   D. fs.removeFile()
   Correct Answer: B. fs.writeFile()
   Explanation:
   writeFile writes new content, creating or overwriting the file. appendFile adds to the end instead of overwriting.

5. **If you need to add data to an existing log file without overwriting, which method do you use?**
   A. `fs.appendFile()`
   B. `fs.writeFile()` with the overwrite flag set to false
   C. `fs.logFile()`
   D. `fs.createWriteStream()` only
   Correct Answer: A. `fs.appendFile()`
   Explanation:
   `appendFile` is specifically designed to add data to the existing content. `writeFile` overwrites by default.
6. **Which method would you call to check file statistics like size, creation time, and whether it's a file or directory?**
   A. `fs.stat()`
   B. `fs.inspect()`
   C. `fs.info()`
   D. `fs.readStats()`
   Correct Answer: A. `fs.stat()`
   Explanation:
   `fs.stat` returns a `Stats` object with properties like `size, mtime, isFile(), isDirectory()`, etc.
7. **Which method removes a file from the file system?**
   A. `fs.unlink()`
   B. `fs.remove()`
   C. `fs.delete()`
   D. `fs.destroyFile()`
   Correct Answer: A. `fs.unlink()`
   Explanation:
   `unlink` is the Node.js method for deleting a file. If the file doesn't exist, it throws an error in the callback/promise.

8. If you use `fs.rename('old.txt', 'new.txt', callback)`, what happens if `old.txt` doesn't exist?
A. It silently creates a new file named `new.txt`
B. It throws an error indicating `old.txt` cannot be found
C. It automatically writes "undefined" to `new.txt`
D. The rename operation is retried until `old.txt` appears
Correct Answer: B. It throws an error indicating `old.txt` cannot be found
Explanation:
`fs.rename` calls the callback with an error if the source file doesn't exist.

9. Which argument do you typically pass to methods like `fs.readFile` to read files as strings instead of Buffer objects?
A. An integer specifying chunk size
B. `'base64'`
C. `'utf8'`
D. `'parseString'`
Correct Answer: C. `'utf8'`
Explanation:
Specifying `'utf8'` as the encoding returns the file content as a string rather than a raw Buffer.

10. Which scenario is not a common use of the Node.js File System (`fs`) module?
A. Logging incoming HTTP requests to a file
B. Reading and writing JSON configurations
C. Managing database queries for relational data
D. Serving static files in a simple server
Correct Answer: C. Managing database queries for relational data
Explanation:
Database queries typically require separate drivers or ORMs. The `fs` module deals with the local file system, not relational databases.

Section 7: Working with Packages

1. **Which command is used to initialize a `package.json` file in a Node.js project interactively?**
   A. `npm init`
   B. `npm config`
   C. `npm setup`
   D. `npm start`
   Correct Answer: A. `npm init`
   Explanation:
   `npm init` prompts you for details like project name, version, description, etc., then creates `package.json`.

2. **What is `chalk` used for in Node.js?**
   A. Handling HTTP requests
   B. Adding color and styles to console output
   C. Managing environment variables
   D. Setting up an Express server
   Correct Answer: B. Adding color and styles to console output
   Explanation:
   `chalk` is a popular library for applying text color, background color, and other styles in the terminal.

3. **Which is not a benefit of using nodemon in development?**
   A. It restarts your Node.js app automatically on file changes
   B. It is used to debug memory leaks automatically
   C. It reduces repetitive manual restarts for changes
   D. It's commonly installed as a dev dependency
   Correct Answer: B. It is used to debug memory leaks automatically
   Explanation:
   nodemon merely watches file changes and restarts the app. It doesn't handle debugging or memory profiling by itself.

4. What does `npm install --save chalk` do in modern npm versions?
   A. Installs chalk globally
   B. Installs chalk in devDependencies
   C. Installs chalk locally and updates dependencies in `package.json`
   D. Uninstalls chalk from your project
   Correct Answer: C. Installs chalk locally and updates dependencies in `package.json`
   Explanation:
   As of npm v5 and above, `--save` is the default for `npm install <package>`. It places the package in `dependencies`.

5. **Which file describes the dependencies you installed, including their exact versions and sub-dependencies, to ensure repeatable installs?**
   A. `package-lock.json`
   B. `node_modules.json`
   C. `dependencies.json`
   D. `package.json`
   Correct Answer: A. `package-lock.json`
   Explanation:
   `package-lock.json` locks the entire dependency tree (including nested packages).

6. **To install a package only for development (not in production), which command do you use?**
   A. `npm install <package>`
   B. `npm uninstall --save-dev <package>`
   C. `npm install --save-dev <package>`
   D. `npm install -g <package>`
   Correct Answer: C. `npm install --save-dev <package>`
   Explanation:
   This places the package under `devDependencies`. They're typically not needed in production.

7. **If you run `npm outdated`, what information do you see?**
   A. The scripts available in `package.json`
   B. The outdated system libraries
   C. Which installed dependencies have newer versions available
   D. A detailed stack trace for any runtime errors
   Correct Answer: C. Which installed dependencies have newer versions available
   Explanation:
   `npm outdated` shows the current, wanted, and latest versions, letting you decide if you want to update.

8. **What is the recommended approach when you no longer need a package in your project?**
   A. Manually delete the folder in `node_modules`
   B. `npm uninstall <package>` to remove it and update `package.json`
   C. Rename the package in `package.json`
   D. The package stays forever even if you don't use it
   Correct Answer: B. `npm uninstall <package>` to remove it and update `package.json`
   Explanation:
   Uninstalling properly removes it from `node_modules` and `dependencies` in `package.json`.

9. **Which file typically contains the script `"start"`: `"node app.js"`?**
   A. `package-lock.json`
   B. `server.js`
   C. `app.json`
   D. `package.json`
   Correct Answer: D. `package.json`
   Explanation:
   You define custom npm scripts in the `scripts` section of `package.json`.

10. **Which is a popular third-party library to perform HTTP requests inside a Node.js app?**
    A. `lodash`
    B. `axios`
    C. `fs`
    D. `http`
    Correct Answer: B. `axios`
    Explanation:
    `axios` is not a core module; it's a third-party library that simplifies HTTP calls, used frequently in both Node.js and browser JavaScript.

Section 8: Introduction to Asynchronous Programming

1. **Which of the following is not a valid state of a JavaScript Promise?**
   A. Pending
   B. Fulfilled
   C. Canceled
   D. Rejected
   Correct Answer: C. Canceled
   Explanation:
   Promises can be pending, fulfilled, or rejected. There is no standard "canceled" state in the native Promise specification.
2. **In Node.js callbacks, what is the typical signature?**
   A. `(result, error) => { ... }`
   B. `(error, data) => { ... }`
   C. `(request, response) => { ... }`
   D. `(then, catch) => { ... }`
   Correct Answer: B. `(error, data) => { ... }`
   Explanation:
   Node.js commonly uses the error-first callback pattern: the first argument is an error (if any), and the second is the result.

3. **Which method is typically used to handle success and errors in promises?**
   A. `.then()` for success, `.catch()` for errors
   B. `.success()` for success, `.error()` for errors
   C. `.resolve()` for success, `.reject()` for errors directly in chain
   D. `.callback()` for success, `.fail()` for errors
   Correct Answer: A. `.then()` for success, `.catch()` for errors
   Explanation:
   JavaScript Promises chain with `.then(res => ...)` for success, and `.catch(err => ...)` for rejections.

4. **Which statement about `async/await` is correct?**
   A. They are a replacement for Node.js callbacks that block the main thread
   B. They are syntactic sugar over promises to write asynchronous code more synchronously
   C. They are older than the promise-based approach
   D. They require multi-threading to function
   Correct Answer: B. They are syntactic sugar over promises to write asynchronous code more synchronously
   Explanation:
   `async/await` internally uses Promises. The code style is more straightforward, but the asynchronous nature remains.

5. **When an error is thrown inside an `async` function without a try/catch block, it becomes...**
   A. A syntax error
   B. A rejected promise
   C. A blocking error that stops all JavaScript execution
   D. An event that must be handled by the Node.js event loop
   Correct Answer: B. A rejected promise
   Explanation:
   Inside `async` functions, unhandled errors translate into promise rejections.

6. **Which is not a typical advantage of promises over callbacks?**
A. They avoid "callback hell" by chaining operations
B. They allow more structured error handling with `.catch`
C. They are synchronous by default
D. They can chain multiple async tasks more cleanly
Correct Answer: C. They are synchronous by default
Explanation:
Promises are asynchronous. They provide a neater approach than deeply nested callbacks.

7. **Which method runs multiple promises in parallel and resolves once all have fulfilled (or rejects if any fail)?**
A. `Promise.race([])`
B. `Promise.all([])`
C. `Promise.allSettled([])`
D. `Promise.any([])`
Correct Answer: B. `Promise.all([])`
Explanation:
`Promise.all` returns an array of results if all promises resolve, or rejects immediately on the first rejection.

8. **If you have `await somePromise`, where can that statement appear?**
A. At the top level of a file without any configuration
B. Only in a function declared with the `async` keyword
C. In any Node.js callback function
D. In synchronous scripts that do not use Node
Correct Answer: B. Only in a function declared with the `async` keyword
Explanation:
The `await` keyword can only be used inside an `async` function (or top-level in an ES module with certain Node versions/flags).

9. In the following code, what is `.then(response =>
   console.log(response))` an example of?
   ```
   myPromiseFunction().then(response =>
   console.log(response));
   ```
   A. Callback function
   B. Promise chain
   C. Synchronous error handling
   D. Immediately Invoked Function Expression
   Correct Answer: B. Promise chain
   Explanation:
   `.then(...)` is part of the promise chaining approach,
   handling the result of `myPromiseFunction()`.
10. **Which method can handle multiple asynchronous
    calls in series without large nesting in code?**
    A. Callback chaining
    B. Single callback with `if-else`
    C. `.then()` chaining in Promises or using
    `async/await` sequentially
    D. A do-while loop with synchronous calls
    **Correct Answer: C. `.then()` chaining in Promises or
    using `async/await` sequentially**
    Explanation:
    Both promise chaining and async/await enable a
    readable series of asynchronous operations.

Section 9: Creating a Simple API

1. **What does an API typically allow you to do?**
   A. Compile front-end code into the browser
   B. Interact with a service or application via defined endpoints for data exchange
   C. Run Node.js scripts without installing Node
   D. Bypass all security checks
   Correct Answer: B. Interact with a service or application via defined endpoints for data exchange
   Explanation:
   An API is a contract that allows clients to send requests and receive responses for specific resources or actions.

2. **Which HTTP method is commonly used to retrieve resources in a RESTful API?**
   A. POST
   B. GET
   C. UPDATE
   D. DELETE
   Correct Answer: B. GET
   Explanation:
   GET is used to fetch or read data from the server. POST is for creation, PUT/PATCH for updating, and DELETE for removal.

3. **What is the appropriate status code to return when creating a new resource via POST is successful?**
   A. 200 OK
   B. 201 Created
   C. 304 Not Modified
   D. 400 Bad Request
   Correct Answer: B. 201 Created
   Explanation:
   In HTTP, `201 Created` indicates that the server successfully created a resource, typically used for POST requests.

4. When building an API with Node's native `http` module, how do you parse JSON data in the request body?
A. Use `req.body` directly in every scenario
B. JSON is parsed automatically by Node.js
C. Manually gather data from `req.on('data')` events, then `JSON.parse` it
D. Node cannot parse JSON
Correct Answer: C. Manually gather data from `req.on('data')` events, then `JSON.parse` it
Explanation:
Without a framework, you must handle the raw data chunks yourself and parse them to get JSON objects.

5. What is the typical approach to handle different routes (e.g., `/api/users`, `/api/products`) in a plain Node.js server?
A. A single route that returns everything
B. Checking `req.url` and `req.method` in conditional statements
C. Using `os` module to parse the endpoint
D. Storing route definitions in `package.json`
Correct Answer: B. Checking `req.url` and `req.method` in conditional statements
Explanation:
You can parse the path from `req.url`, compare it in if-else or switch, and handle logic for each endpoint.

6. Which tool is commonly used to test APIs by sending HTTP requests (GET, POST, etc.)?
A. npm CLI
B. Node.js REPL
C. Postman or similar HTTP client (e.g., Insomnia)
D. Visual Studio Code's extension manager
Correct Answer: C. Postman or similar HTTP client (e.g., Insomnia)
Explanation:
Postman (or alternatives) let you craft custom requests to your API, specifying headers, body, etc.

7. **Which response header is important when returning JSON from an API endpoint?**

   A. `Content-Type: application/json`

   B. `Content-Length: 0`

   C. `Transfer-Encoding: chunked`

   D. `X-Powered-By: Node.js`

   Correct Answer: A. `Content-Type: application/json`

   Explanation:

   This informs the client that the response should be interpreted as JSON data.

8. **What does an HTTP 404 status code indicate?**

   A. The request is accepted for processing but not completed

   B. The resource or endpoint is not found

   C. An internal server error occurred

   D. A new resource was successfully created

   Correct Answer: B. The resource or endpoint is not found

   Explanation:

   404 is the standard "Not Found" code if the endpoint or resource does not exist on the server.

9. **Which method is primarily used to create or insert new data in RESTful APIs?**

   A. GET

   B. POST

   C. PATCH

   D. DELETE

   Correct Answer: B. POST

   Explanation:

   POST is used to submit an entity to the specified resource, causing a new resource to be created.

10. **When building a simple Node.js API, what is the recommended step for testing JSON responses in your browser's console?**
A. Using
`alert(JSON.stringify(fetch('/api/...')))`
B. Using the `fetch` API in the DevTools console to request your API
C. Disabling CORS at the OS level
D. Running `npm test` automatically detects and logs JSON
Correct Answer: B. Using the `fetch` API in the DevTools console to request your API
Explanation:
You can open DevTools, type
`fetch('http://localhost:3000/api/...').then(res => res.json()).then(data => console.log(data))` to view the response.

Section 10: Next Steps and Learning Resources

1. **Which Node.js framework is known for simplifying server creation, routing, and middleware?**
A. Express.js
B. Mongoose
C. PostgreSQL
D. React.js
Correct Answer: A. Express.js
Explanation:
Express is a minimal framework that makes building HTTP servers more convenient with routing and middleware concepts.

2. **What is a common next step after learning the Node.js basics?**
A. Avoid using databases and handle everything in memory only
B. Learn about frameworks like Express.js, connect a database (e.g., MongoDB), and build real projects
C. Only create static files in Node
D. Rewrite all server code in Python
Correct Answer: B. Learn about frameworks like Express.js, connect a database (e.g., MongoDB), and build real projects
Explanation:
This route helps you apply Node.js knowledge to production-ready applications, typical in modern web development.

3. **Why might a new Node.js developer explore MongoDB as a database option?**
A. It's a strict relational database requiring complex SQL
B. It's a popular NoSQL database, easy for beginners to store JSON-like documents
C. It only works with front-end code
D. It doesn't require learning any queries
Correct Answer: B. It's a popular NoSQL database, easy for beginners to store JSON-like documents
Explanation:
MongoDB is friendly to JavaScript developers since documents are similar to JSON objects.

4. **Which resource is an official place to learn about Node.js APIs and updates?**
A. randomnodejs.org
B. Official Node.js documentation at https://nodejs.org/en/docs/
C. Only the Node.js source code on GitHub
D. Online code snippet websites with no official credentials
Correct Answer: B. Official Node.js documentation at https://nodejs.org/en/docs/
Explanation:
The official docs detail Node.js core modules, upcoming changes, and best practices.

5. **Which project idea can help beginners practice CRUD operations in Node.js?**
A. A static landing page without any interactions
B. A to-do list app with database for tasks
C. A WordPress theme for blogs
D. A React native mobile app
Correct Answer: B. A to-do list app with database for tasks
Explanation:
A to-do list is a classic example for learning create, read, update, and delete flows with Node.js + database.

6. **What is Express middleware?**
A. A function with signature (`req, res, next`) that can process requests before the final route handler
B. A database driver for Node.js
C. A tool for debugging memory leaks in Node
D. The main `index.js` file in an Express app
Correct Answer: A. A function with signature (`req, res, next`) that can process requests before the final route handler
Explanation:
Middleware can parse request bodies, handle authentication, log requests, or process data before sending a response or calling `next()`.

7. **Which library is commonly used with MongoDB to define schemas and models in Node.js?**
   A. Express
   B. Lodash
   C. Mongoose
   D. Chalk
   Correct Answer: C. Mongoose
   Explanation:
   Mongoose is an Object Data Modeling (ODM) library for MongoDB, letting you define model schemas and work with queries in Node.js.
8. **Which statement best describes a "practice project" for beginners?**
   A. An advanced project that requires microservices architecture
   B. A smaller, focused application that helps you apply Node.js concepts in a practical way
   C. A production-ready system with thousands of lines of code
   D. A project that must use only synchronous file operations
   Correct Answer: B. A smaller, focused application that helps you apply Node.js concepts in a practical way
   Explanation:
   Practice projects let you learn by doing, building smaller-scale apps to experiment with Node.js features.

9. **Which resource might you consult for advanced Node.js topics like clustering, security, or performance?**
A. Official Node.js documentation, advanced guides, specialized courses
B. Only the older versions of Node.js blog posts
C. Rare hardware manuals
D. None, since Node.js can't handle advanced tasks
Correct Answer: A. Official Node.js documentation, advanced guides, specialized courses
Explanation:
Official docs and specialized online resources delve into advanced usage: clustering, streams, scaling, and more.

10. **Which statement about continuing your Node.js education is true?**
A. Once you know the basics, there is nothing else to learn
B. Learning frameworks (like Express), databases, testing, and best practices can significantly advance your skills
C. Node.js is only suitable for small scripts
D. Node.js is obsolete and replaced by browsers
Correct Answer: B. Learning frameworks (like Express), databases, testing, and best practices can significantly advance your skills
Explanation:
Node.js is widely used in production for diverse applications. Progressing beyond basics to frameworks, DB integration, testing, and advanced patterns is essential for professional Node.js development.

Concluding Note

These **100 multiple-choice questions** span the key lessons from:

Use them to gauge your understanding of Node.js basics, the event-driven architecture, npm ecosystem, file system operations, building and testing simple APIs, and directions for further study—like Express.js or database integration. Good luck refining your Node.js expertise!

Coding Exercises

Section 1: Introduction to Node.js

In these exercises, you'll explore fundamental Node.js concepts—running JavaScript outside the browser, using the REPL, and understanding Node's single-threaded nature.

Exercise 1.1: Hello World (Console)

Objective: Validate that Node is installed and can run a simple script.

```
// helloWorld.js
console.log("Hello World from Node.js!");
```

Run:

```
node helloWorld.js
```

Outcome: Logs the message to your terminal.

Exercise 1.2: Version Check

Objective: Practice reading system info in Node.

```
// versionCheck.js
console.log("Node version:",
process.version);
console.log("Operating system:",
process.platform);
```

Run:

```
node versionCheck.js
```

Outcome: Prints Node.js version and OS type.

Exercise 1.3: Using the REPL

Objective: Perform basic arithmetic in the Node.js REPL.

Open your terminal and type:

```
node
```
Type:

```
> 2 + 3
> const greeting = "Hello from the REPL!";
> greeting
```

1. Type .exit to leave.

Outcome: You interactively see evaluations of expressions without creating a file.

Exercise 1.4: Single Thread Demonstration

Objective: Show non-blocking vs. blocking behavior with setTimeout.

```
// singleThread.js
console.log("Start");
setTimeout(() => {
  console.log("Async message after 1
second");
}, 1000);
console.log("End");
```

Run:

```
node singleThread.js
```

Outcome: "End" logs before the delayed message, illustrating asynchronous behavior.

Exercise 1.5: Command-Line Arguments

Objective: Access arguments from process.argv.

```
// greetArg.js
const args = process.argv.slice(2); // skip
first two default entries
const name = args[0] || "Stranger";
console.log(`Hello, ${name}!`);
```

Run:

```
node greetArg.js Alice
```

Outcome: Logs "Hello, Alice!" if you provide "Alice" as an argument.

Exercise 1.6: Basic Module Export

Objective: Practice splitting logic into two files.

```
// myModule.js
function sayHello() {
  return "Hello from a custom module!";
}
module.exports = sayHello;
// useModule.js
const greet = require('./myModule');
console.log(greet());
```

Run:

```
node useModule.js
```

Outcome: Confirms you can require your own module.

Exercise 1.7: Exploring process Object

Objective: Print current working directory, PID, and other process info.

```
// processInfo.js
console.log("PID:", process.pid);
console.log("Current Working Directory:",
process.cwd());
console.log("Node.js Version:",
process.version);
```

Outcome: Useful for debugging or logging environment information.

Exercise 1.8: Simple Timer

Objective: Explore setInterval and clearInterval.

```
// timerDemo.js
let count = 0;
const intervalId = setInterval(() => {
  count++;
  console.log(`Count is: ${count}`);
  if (count >= 5) {
    console.log("Done counting.");
    clearInterval(intervalId);
  }
}, 1000);
```

Outcome: Prints a count every second, stopping at 5.

Exercise 1.9: Handling Environment Variables

Objective: Use environment variables in Node.

```
// envDemo.js
const port = process.env.PORT || 3000;
console.log(`Using port: ${port}`);
```

Run:

```
PORT=4000 node envDemo.js
```

Outcome: Logs the port, defaulting to 3000 if none is specified.

Exercise 1.10: Checking Non-Blocking Behavior

Objective: Show that Node can continue execution while an async function is pending.

```
// asyncBehavior.js
function asyncOperation(callback) {
  setTimeout(() => {
```

```
    callback("Data loaded!");
  }, 2000);
}
console.log("Before");
asyncOperation((message) => {
  console.log("Message from asyncOperation:",
message);
});
console.log("After");
```

Outcome: "After" logs before the async callback, confirming non-blocking operations.

Section 2: Setting Up Node.js

These exercises guide you through initializing a project, configuring package.json, installing packages, and verifying versions.

Exercise 2.1: Verify Node and npm Versions

Objective: Confirm Node.js & npm are installed.

```
node -v
npm -v
```

Outcome: Displays version numbers if installed.

Exercise 2.2: Initialize a Project

Objective: Create a package.json file.

```
mkdir project-exercise2
cd project-exercise2
npm init -y
```

Outcome: Generates a default `package.json` with your project info.

Exercise 2.3: Inspect package.json

Objective: Open and explore the file:

1. Check fields: `"name"`, `"version"`, `"scripts"`, etc.

Add a custom script:

```
{
  "scripts": {
    "start": "node index.js"
  }
}
```

Outcome: Understanding how `package.json` is structured.

Exercise 2.4: Local vs. Global Installation

Objective: Install a package locally vs. globally.

Local:

```
npm install chalk
```
Global:

```
npm install -g nodemon
```

Outcome: Distinguish local (`node_modules` in the project) from global installs.

Exercise 2.5: Creating a Simple Script

Objective: Use a custom npm script to run your app.

```
// index.js
console.log("Running index.js via npm
script!");
```

In `package.json`:

```
{
  "scripts": {
    "dev": "node index.js"
  }
}
```

Run:

```
npm run dev
```

Outcome: Simplifies running your code.

Exercise 2.6: Checking Outdated Packages

Objective: Show how to update dependencies.

Install an older version of a package, e.g.:

```
npm install chalk@4.1.2
```
Check for updates:

```
npm outdated
```

Outcome: Practice seeing available updates for your installed packages.

Exercise 2.7: Creating a Global CLI Shortcut

Objective: Create a script that can be run globally (requires a bit of setup).

```
#!/usr/bin/env node
console.log("Hello from a global CLI tool!");
```

1. Add this file to a folder, e.g., `bin/cli-demo.js`.

Add to `package.json`:

```
{
  "bin": {
    "cli-demo": "./bin/cli-demo.js"
  }
}
```
Install globally:

```
npm install -g .
```

Outcome: Run `cli-demo` from anywhere.

Exercise 2.8: Using nvm (Node Version Manager)

Objective: Switch between different Node versions (conceptual, commands only).

1. **Install** nvm (depends on OS).

Install a new Node version:

```
nvm install 14
```
Switch to that version:

```
nvm use 14
```

Outcome: Confirm you can switch Node versions easily.

Exercise 2.9: Adding Keywords/Author in package.json

Objective: Provide metadata for your project.

```
npm init
```

Answer the prompts thoroughly. Or manually edit package.json to add:

```json
{
  "name": "my-awesome-project",
  "version": "1.0.0",
  "author": "Your Name",
  "keywords": ["node", "learning",
"beginners"]
}
```

Outcome: This metadata is used for npm searches and clarity about project ownership.

Exercise 2.10: Publishing a Test Package (Optional)

Objective: Publish a simple package to npm (requires npm account).

1. **Add** a simple script or library file.

Log in:

```
npm login
```
Publish:

```
npm publish
```

Outcome: Make your package available publicly (or privately) via npm.

Section 3: Writing Your First Node.js Program

These exercises reinforce REPL usage, console logging, command-line arguments, and file-based scripts.

Exercise 3.1: Basic Input/Output

Objective: Accept user input from `process.stdin`.

```
// readStdin.js
process.stdout.write("What's your name? ");
process.stdin.on('data', (data) => {
  const name = data.toString().trim();
  console.log(`Hello, ${name}!`);
  process.exit();
});
```

Run:

```
node readStdin.js
```

Outcome: Waits for user input, then greets them.

Exercise 3.2: Simple Math Operation

Objective: Accept two numbers from command-line arguments and add them.

```
// addNumbers.js
const args = process.argv.slice(2);
const num1 = parseInt(args[0], 10);
const num2 = parseInt(args[1], 10);
console.log(`Sum: ${num1 + num2}`);
```

Outcome: For example, `node addNumbers.js 5 7` => `Sum: 12`.

Exercise 3.3: REPL Arithmetic

Objective: Use the REPL to test arithmetic without a file.

1. **Type** `node` in your terminal.

Enter:

```
> let x = 10;
> x * 3
30
> .exit
```

Outcome: Quick calculations without writing a script.

Exercise 3.4: Multi-Line String (ES6 Template Literal)

Objective: Show how to format multiline outputs.

```
// multiline.js
const message = `
  Hello,
  This is a multi-line
  string in Node.js
`;
console.log(message);
```

Outcome: The console prints each line with the original formatting.

Exercise 3.5: Node.js Command-Line Flag

Objective: Demonstrate a simple CLI flag approach.

```
// cliFlag.js
const args = process.argv.slice(2);
if (args.includes('--version')) {
  console.log("Version 1.0.0");
} else {
  console.log("Run with --version to see
version info.");
}
```

Run:

```
node cliFlag.js --version
```

Outcome: Prints version if `--version` flag is present.

Exercise 3.6: REPL Custom Command

Objective: Use the `.help` command in the REPL to discover built-in commands.

Type:

```
node
> .help
```

1. Explore `.break`, `.exit`, etc. **Outcome**: Familiarity with special REPL commands.

Exercise 3.7: Conditionals in Node.js

Objective: Basic if-else logic in a Node script.

```
// checkNumber.js
```

```
const num = parseInt(process.argv[2], 10);
if (num > 10) {
  console.log("Number is greater than 10");
} else {
  console.log("Number is 10 or less");
}
```

Outcome: A basic demonstration of conditional statements.

Exercise 3.8: Synchronous Script

Objective: Show a synchronous operation (like reading a small file) for demonstration.

```
// syncRead.js
const fs = require('fs');
const data = fs.readFileSync('example.txt',
'utf8');
console.log("File contents:", data);
```

Outcome: The script blocks until example.txt is read.

Exercise 3.9: Simple Logging to a File

Objective: Minimal demonstration of Node's fs usage (still in "writing your first program").

```
// logToFile.js
const fs = require('fs');
fs.writeFileSync('log.txt', 'First log
entry!\n', { flag: 'a' });
console.log("Log entry added.");
```

Outcome: Appends text to log.txt.

Exercise 3.10: Using console.error

Objective: Differentiate `console.log` vs. `console.error`.

```
// errorDemo.js
console.log("Info: This is a normal log");
console.error("Error: Something went
wrong!");
```

Outcome: Shows how error logs can be redirected separately (e.g., in shells).

Section 4: Node.js Core Modules

Focus on the `fs`, `path`, `os`, `http`, and other built-in modules.

Exercise 4.1: Reading a File (Asynchronous)

```
// readFileAsync.js
const fs = require('fs');
fs.readFile('sample.txt', 'utf8', (err, data)
=> {
  if (err) {
    return console.error("Read error:", err);
  }
  console.log("File contents:", data);
});
```

Outcome: Logs file contents after reading completes.

Exercise 4.2: Writing a File (Asynchronous)

```
// writeFileAsync.js
const fs = require('fs');
const content = "Hello, this is an async
write!";
```

```javascript
fs.writeFile('output.txt', content, (err) =>
{
  if (err) {
    return console.error("Write error:",
err);
  }
  console.log("File written successfully!");
});
```

Outcome: Creates/overwrites output.txt with specified content.

Exercise 4.3: Building a Path with path.join

```javascript
// pathJoin.js
const path = require('path');
const dir = 'folder';
const file = 'test.txt';
const fullPath = path.join(__dirname, dir,
file);
console.log("Full path:", fullPath);
```

Outcome: Prints a normalized path (correct for your OS).

Exercise 4.4: Parse a Path

```javascript
// pathParse.js
const path = require('path');
const filePath =
'/home/user/projects/demo/app.js';
const parsed = path.parse(filePath);
console.log("Parsed path:", parsed);
```

Outcome: Logs an object with root, dir, base, ext, name.

Exercise 4.5: Checking OS Info

```
// osInfo.js
const os = require('os');
console.log("Platform:", os.platform());
console.log("CPU architecture:", os.arch());
console.log("CPUs:", os.cpus());
console.log("Free Memory:", os.freemem());
```

Outcome: Displays system info.

Exercise 4.6: Basic HTTP Server (Core http)

```
// basicHttp.js
const http = require('http');
const server = http.createServer((req, res)
=> {
  res.writeHead(200, { 'Content-Type':
'text/plain' });
  res.end("Hello from Node's http module!");
});
server.listen(3000, () => {
  console.log("Server running at
http://localhost:3000");
});
```

Outcome: Minimal "Hello World" server at port 3000.

Exercise 4.7: HTTP JSON Response

```
// httpJson.js
const http = require('http');
const server = http.createServer((req, res)
=> {
  const data = { status: 'OK', message:
'Hello JSON' };
```

```
  res.writeHead(200, { 'Content-Type':
'application/json' });
  res.end(JSON.stringify(data));
});
server.listen(3001, () => {
  console.log("JSON server at
http://localhost:3001");
});
```

Outcome: Responds with JSON.

Exercise 4.8: Spawning a Child Process

```
// childProcessDemo.js
const { spawn } = require('child_process');
const ls = spawn('ls', ['-l']);
ls.stdout.on('data', (data) => {
  console.log(`Output: ${data}`);
});
ls.stderr.on('data', (data) => {
  console.error(`Error: ${data}`);
});
ls.on('close', (code) => {
  console.log(`Child process exited with
code: ${code}`);
});
```

Outcome: Executes `ls -l` on Unix-based systems (use `dir` on Windows) and logs output.

Exercise 4.9: Using events Module

```
// eventsDemo.js
const EventEmitter = require('events');
const emitter = new EventEmitter();
```

```
emitter.on('greet', (name) => {
  console.log(`Hello, ${name}!`);
});
emitter.emit('greet', 'Node.js User');
```

Outcome: Demonstrates custom event emission and handling.

Exercise 4.10: Creating a Basic TLS Server (Optional)

```
// tlsServer.js
const https = require('https');
const fs = require('fs');
const options = {
  key: fs.readFileSync('key.pem'),
  cert: fs.readFileSync('cert.pem')
};
https.createServer(options, (req, res) => {
  res.writeHead(200);
  res.end("Hello over HTTPS!");
}).listen(3443, () => {
  console.log("HTTPS server on
https://localhost:3443");
});
```

Outcome: Only works if you have valid certificate files, but demonstrates https usage.

Section 5: Building a Simple HTTP Server

Focus on creation of servers, responding to routes, sending plain text or JSON, and so on.

Exercise 5.1: Basic Plain Text Server

```
// plainTextServer.js
const http = require('http');
const server = http.createServer((req, res)
=> {
  res.writeHead(200, { 'Content-Type':
'text/plain' });
  res.end("Hello from a simple HTTP
server!");
});
server.listen(3000, () => console.log("Server
at http://localhost:3000"));
```

Outcome: Minimal server returning plain text.

Exercise 5.2: Serving Different Routes

```
// multiRouteServer.js
const http = require('http');
const server = http.createServer((req, res)
=> {
  if (req.url === '/' && req.method ===
'GET') {
    res.writeHead(200, { 'Content-Type':
'text/plain' });
    res.end("Home Page");
  } else if (req.url === '/about' &&
req.method === 'GET') {
    res.writeHead(200, { 'Content-Type':
'text/plain' });
    res.end("About Page");
  } else {
    res.writeHead(404);
    res.end("Not Found");
  }
```

```
});
server.listen(3001, () => console.log("Routes
server at http://localhost:3001"));
```

Outcome: Different text depending on the path.

Exercise 5.3: Serving JSON

```
// jsonServer.js
const http = require('http');
const server = http.createServer((req, res)
=> {
  const response = { status: 'success', data:
[1, 2, 3] };
  res.writeHead(200, { 'Content-Type':
'application/json' });
  res.end(JSON.stringify(response));
});
server.listen(3002, () => console.log("JSON
server at http://localhost:3002"));
```

Outcome: Returns a JSON object with status and data.

Exercise 5.4: Handling POST Data

```
// postHandler.js
const http = require('http');
const server = http.createServer((req, res)
=> {
  if (req.url === '/data' && req.method ===
'POST') {
    let body = '';
    req.on('data', chunk => body += chunk);
    req.on('end', () => {
      const parsed = JSON.parse(body);
```

```
      res.writeHead(200, { 'Content-Type':
'application/json' });
      res.end(JSON.stringify({ received:
parsed }));
    });
  } else {
    res.writeHead(404);
    res.end();
  }
});
server.listen(3003, () => console.log("POST
handler at http://localhost:3003"));
```

Outcome: Responds with the JSON you send in the request body.

Exercise 5.5: Logging Requests

```
// logRequests.js
const http = require('http');
const server = http.createServer((req, res)
=> {
  console.log(`Incoming request:
${req.method} ${req.url}`);
  res.writeHead(200, { 'Content-Type':
'text/plain' });
  res.end("Request logged");
});
server.listen(3004, () => console.log("Log
server at http://localhost:3004"));
```

Outcome: Logs each request method and URL to the console.

Exercise 5.6: Returning Different Status Codes

```
// statusCodes.js
const http = require('http');
const server = http.createServer((req, res)
=> {
  if (req.url === '/accepted') {
    res.writeHead(202);
    res.end("Request accepted");
  } else if (req.url === '/not-found') {
    res.writeHead(404);
    res.end("Resource not found");
  } else {
    res.writeHead(200);
    res.end("Default response");
  }
});
server.listen(3005, () => console.log("Status
server at http://localhost:3005"));
```

Outcome: Showcases 202 and 404 codes based on URLs.

Exercise 5.7: Serving Static HTML (Minimal)

```
// staticHtmlServer.js
const http = require('http');
const fs = require('fs');
const path = require('path');
const server = http.createServer((req, res)
=> {
  if (req.url === '/') {
    const filePath = path.join(__dirname,
'index.html');
    fs.readFile(filePath, (err, data) => {
      if (err) {
        res.writeHead(500);
```

```
      return res.end("Error loading file");
    }
    res.writeHead(200, { 'Content-Type':
'text/html' });
    res.end(data);
  });
  } else {
    res.writeHead(404);
    res.end("Not Found");
  }
});
server.listen(3006, () => console.log("Static
server at http://localhost:3006"));
```

Outcome: Returns index.html when hitting the root URL.

Exercise 5.8: Query Strings in a GET Request

```
// queryParams.js
const http = require('http');
const url = require('url');
const server = http.createServer((req, res)
=> {
  const parsedUrl = url.parse(req.url, true);
  if (parsedUrl.pathname === '/greet' &&
req.method === 'GET') {
    const name = parsedUrl.query.name ||
'Stranger';
    res.writeHead(200, { 'Content-Type':
'text/plain' });
    res.end(`Hello, ${name}!`);
  } else {
    res.writeHead(404);
    res.end("Not Found");
  }
```

```
});
server.listen(3007, () => console.log("Query
server at http://localhost:3007"));
```

Outcome: GET /greet?name=Alice => "Hello, Alice!"

Exercise 5.9: Simple HTML Form Handling (POST)

```
// formHandler.js
const http = require('http');
const htmlForm = `
<!DOCTYPE html>
<html>
<head><title>Form</title></head>
<body>
  <form method="POST" action="/">
    <input type="text" name="message" />
    <button type="submit">Submit</button>
  </form>
</body>
</html>
`;
const server = http.createServer((req, res)
=> {
  if (req.method === 'GET') {
    res.writeHead(200, { 'Content-Type':
'text/html' });
    res.end(htmlForm);
  } else if (req.method === 'POST') {
    let body = '';
    req.on('data', chunk => (body += chunk));
    req.on('end', () => {
      res.writeHead(200, { 'Content-Type':
'text/plain' });
```

```
      res.end(`Received form data: ${body}`);
    });
  } else {
    res.writeHead(404).end();
  }
});
server.listen(3008, () => console.log("Form
server at http://localhost:3008"));
```

Outcome: Accepts a simple POST submission from an HTML form.

Exercise 5.10: Graceful Shutdown

```
// gracefulShutdown.js
const http = require('http');
const server = http.createServer((req, res)
=> {
  res.end("Hello with graceful shutdown!");
});
server.listen(3009, () => console.log("Server
at http://localhost:3009"));
process.on('SIGINT', () => {
  console.log("\nReceived SIGINT, shutting
down...");
  server.close(() => {
    console.log("Server closed.");
    process.exit(0);
  });
});
```

Outcome: Press Ctrl + C => logs shutdown sequence and closes server gracefully.

Section 6: Working with the File System

Further emphasis on file read/write, directories, and logs.

Exercise 6.1: Read File Synchronously

```
// syncRead.js
const fs = require('fs');
try {
  const data = fs.readFileSync('test.txt',
'utf8');
  console.log("File content:", data);
} catch (err) {
  console.error("Error:", err);
}
```

Outcome: Blocks until reading is complete, logs content or error.

Exercise 6.2: Append Log File

```
// appendLog.js
const fs = require('fs');
const logEntry = `Log entry at ${new
Date().toISOString()}\n`;
fs.appendFile('log.txt', logEntry, (err) => {
  if (err) return console.error("Error:",
err);
  console.log("Log entry appended!");
});
```

Outcome: Appends a timestamped entry to log.txt.

Exercise 6.3: Create a Directory

```
// createDir.js
const fs = require('fs');
fs.mkdir('myNewDir', (err) => {
  if (err) {
    return console.error("Error creating
directory:", err);
  }
  console.log("Directory created: myNewDir");
});
```

Outcome: Creates a new directory named myNewDir.

Exercise 6.4: Remove a File

```
// removeFile.js
const fs = require('fs');
fs.unlink('fileToRemove.txt', (err) => {
  if (err) {
    return console.error("Error deleting
file:", err);
  }
  console.log("File removed successfully!");
});
```

Outcome: Deletes fileToRemove.txt if it exists.

Exercise 6.5: Rename a File

```
// renameFile.js
const fs = require('fs');
fs.rename('oldName.txt', 'newName.txt', (err)
=> {
  if (err) {
```

```
    return console.error("Rename error:",
err);
  }
  console.log("File renamed successfully!");
});
```

Outcome: Changes oldName.txt to newName.txt.

Exercise 6.6: List Files in a Directory

```
// listFiles.js
const fs = require('fs');
fs.readdir('.', (err, files) => {
  if (err) {
    return console.error("Error reading
dir:", err);
  }
  console.log("Files in current directory:",
files);
});
```

Outcome: Prints array of file/folder names in the current directory.

Exercise 6.7: Checking Stats

```
// fileStats.js
const fs = require('fs');
fs.stat('example.txt', (err, stats) => {
  if (err) {
    return console.error("Stat error:", err);
  }
  console.log("Is file:", stats.isFile());
  console.log("Size in bytes:", stats.size);
});
```

Outcome: Displays metadata (size, isFile, etc.) about
`example.txt`.

Exercise 6.8: Watch a File for Changes

```
// watchFile.js
const fs = require('fs');
fs.watch('watchMe.txt', (eventType, filename)
=> {
  console.log(`${filename} file changed!
Event:`, eventType);
});
console.log("Watching watchMe.txt for
changes...");
```

Outcome: Logs a message whenever `watchMe.txt` is
modified.

Exercise 6.9: Copy a File

```
// copyFile.js
const fs = require('fs');
fs.copyFile('source.txt', 'dest.txt', (err)
=> {
  if (err) return console.error("Copy
error:", err);
  console.log("File copied from source.txt to
dest.txt");
});
```

Outcome: Creates an identical copy of `source.txt` named
`dest.txt`.

Exercise 6.10: Read Directory Recursively (Optional)

```
// readDirRecursive.js
const fs = require('fs');
const path = require('path');
function readDirectory(dirPath) {
  fs.readdir(dirPath, { withFileTypes: true
}, (err, entries) => {
    if (err) return console.error("Error:",
err);
    entries.forEach(entry => {
      const fullPath = path.join(dirPath,
entry.name);
      if (entry.isDirectory()) {
        console.log("Dir:", fullPath);
        readDirectory(fullPath);
      } else {
        console.log("File:", fullPath);
      }
    });
  });
}
readDirectory('.');
```

Outcome: Traverses subfolders, listing directories and files.

Section 7: Working with Packages

Exercises about npm scripts, local & global installs, chalk, nodemon, etc.

Exercise 7.1: Installing Chalk (Local)

```
// chalkExample.js
const chalk = require('chalk');
```

```
console.log(chalk.green("Hello, I'm green
text!"));
console.log(chalk.bgMagenta("Magenta
background!"));
```

Install:

```
npm install chalk
```

Outcome: Terminal output with colorful text.

Exercise 7.2: Using nodemon Locally

Objective:

Install nodemon as dev dependency:

```
npm install --save-dev nodemon
```
Add a script in package.json:

```
{
  "scripts": {
    "start": "nodemon server.js"
  }
}
```

1. **Outcome**: Whenever you edit server.js, nodemon restarts automatically.

Exercise 7.3: Testing an npm Script

```
// scriptDemo.js
console.log("Running scriptDemo!");
```

In package.json:

```
{
```

```
  "scripts": {
    "demo": "node scriptDemo.js"
  }
}
```

Run:

```
npm run demo
```

Outcome: Demonstrates custom npm script usage.

Exercise 7.4: Creating a Package Lock

Objective: Show how `package-lock.json` is generated.

Initialize a new folder:

```
mkdir lock-demo && cd lock-demo
npm init -y
```
Install any package:

```
npm install lodash
```

Outcome: A `package-lock.json` file is created with exact version dependencies.

Exercise 7.5: Outdated and Update

```
# Install older version
npm install chalk@4.1.2
# Check outdated
npm outdated
# Update
npm update chalk
```

Outcome: You see how `npm outdated` shows available updates, and `npm update` brings them current.

Exercise 7.6: Uninstall a Package

```
npm uninstall chalk
```

Outcome: Removes `chalk` from `node_modules` and dependencies in `package.json`.

Exercise 7.7: Global Installation

```
npm install -g serve
```

Run:

```
serve --version
```

Outcome: `serve` can be used from anywhere to serve static files.

Exercise 7.8: Publishing a Scoped Package (Optional)

Objective: If you have an npm account, create a scoped package @yourname/pkg-demo.

Login:

```
npm login
```
In `package.json`:

```
{
  "name": "@yourname/pkg-demo",
  "version": "1.0.0"
}
```

Publish:

```
npm publish --access public
```

Outcome: Package is published under your npm scope.

Exercise 7.9: Explore Package Scripts

Objective: Add multiple scripts in `package.json`.

```
{
  "scripts": {
    "start": "node index.js",
    "dev": "nodemon index.js",
    "test": "echo 'No tests yet'"
  }
}
```

Outcome: Notice how you can define multiple tasks.

Exercise 7.10: Local vs. Global CLI Tools

Objective:

Install `http-server` locally:

```
npm install http-server
```
Run:

```
npx http-server
```

Outcome: With npm@5.2+, `npx` can run local executables without a global install.

Section 8: Introduction to Asynchronous Programming

Exercises on callbacks, promises, async/await, etc.

Exercise 8.1: Simple Callback

```javascript
// callbackDemo.js
function fetchData(callback) {
  setTimeout(() => {
    callback(null, "Fetched data!");
  }, 1000);
}
fetchData((err, data) => {
  if (err) return console.error("Error:",
err);
  console.log("Success:", data);
});
```

Outcome: "Success: Fetched data!" after 1 second.

Exercise 8.2: Error-First Callback

```javascript
// callbackError.js
function getUser(id, callback) {
  setTimeout(() => {
    if (id <= 0) {
      return callback("Invalid ID", null);
    }
    callback(null, { id, name: "Alice" });
  }, 500);
}
getUser(-1, (err, user) => {
  if (err) return console.error("Error:",
err);
```

```
    console.log("User:", user);
});
```

Outcome: Logs an error if ID is invalid.

Exercise 8.3: Promise Example

```
// promiseExample.js
function getData() {
  return new Promise((resolve, reject) => {
    setTimeout(() => {
      resolve("Promise resolved data!");
    }, 700);
  });
}
getData()
  .then(result => console.log(result))
  .catch(err => console.error("Error:",
err));
```

Outcome: Logs the resolved data after 700ms.

Exercise 8.4: Promise Chain

```
// promiseChain.js
function step(message) {
  return new Promise(resolve => {
    setTimeout(() => {
      resolve(message + " -> next");
    }, 300);
  });
}
step("Start")
  .then(res => step(res))
  .then(res => step(res))
```

```
.then(final => console.log("Chained
result:", final));
```

Outcome: Demonstrates sequential promise chaining.

Exercise 8.5: Async/Await Example

```
// asyncAwait.js
function delay(ms) {
  return new Promise(resolve =>
setTimeout(resolve, ms));
}
async function main() {
  console.log("Before await");
  await delay(1000);
  console.log("After 1 second");
}
main();
```

Outcome: Logs two messages with a 1-second pause in between.

Exercise 8.6: Async/Await Error Handling

```
// asyncAwaitError.js
function failSometimes() {
  return new Promise((resolve, reject) => {
    if (Math.random() > 0.5)
resolve("Success!");
    elsc reject("Random Failure");
  });
}
async function run() {
  try {
    const msg = await failSometimes();
```

```
    console.log("Message:", msg);
  } catch (err) {
    console.error("Error caught:", err);
  }
}
run();
```

Outcome: 50% of the time, logs success; otherwise logs an error.

Exercise 8.7: Promise.all

```
// promiseAll.js
function createDelay(msg, ms) {
  return new Promise(resolve => {
    setTimeout(() => resolve(msg), ms);
  });
}
Promise.all([
  createDelay("One", 500),
  createDelay("Two", 300),
  createDelay("Three", 700)
])
.then(results => {
  console.log("All done:", results);
});
```

Outcome: Waits for all tasks, then logs ["One", "Two", "Three"].

Exercise 8.8: Promise.race

```
// promiseRace.js
function quickTask() {
```

```
    return new Promise(resolve => setTimeout(()
=> resolve("Quick!"), 200));
}
function slowTask() {
    return new Promise(resolve => setTimeout(()
=> resolve("Slow!"), 600));
}
Promise.race([quickTask(), slowTask()])
    .then(winner => console.log("Race winner:",
winner));
```

Outcome: Logs "Quick!" because it finishes first.

Exercise 8.9: Converting a Callback to a Promise

```
// callbackToPromise.js
function callbackStyle(cb) {
    setTimeout(() => cb(null, "Old callback
data"), 400);
}
function promiseStyle() {
    return new Promise((resolve, reject) => {
        callbackStyle((err, data) => {
            if (err) reject(err);
            else resolve(data);
        });
    });
}
promiseStyle()
    .then(res => console.log("Converted to
promise:", res))
    .catch(err => console.error(err));
```

Outcome: Demonstrates wrapping callback logic in a promise.

Exercise 8.10: Using setInterval with Async/Await (Trick)

```
// asyncInterval.js
function sleep(ms) {
  return new Promise(resolve =>
setTimeout(resolve, ms));
}
(async function() {
  let count = 0;
  while (count < 5) {
    console.log("Count:", count);
    await sleep(1000);
    count++;
  }
  console.log("Done");
})();
```

Outcome: Logs count every second, using async/await instead of setInterval.

Section 9: Creating a Simple API

These exercises show building endpoints (GET, POST) using Node's http module or a minimal approach.

Exercise 9.1: Basic GET Endpoint (Returning JSON)

```
// apiGet.js
const http = require('http');
const data = { message: "Hello from a simple
API" };
const server = http.createServer((req, res)
=> {
```

```
  if (req.url === '/api' && req.method ===
'GET') {
    res.writeHead(200, { 'Content-Type':
'application/json' });
    res.end(JSON.stringify(data));
  } else {
    res.writeHead(404);
    res.end("Not Found");
  }
});
server.listen(3000, () => console.log("API
server at http://localhost:3000"));
```

Outcome: A minimal JSON endpoint at /api.

Exercise 9.2: Handling POST for JSON Data

```
// apiPost.js
const http = require('http');
let items = [];
const server = http.createServer((req, res)
=> {
  if (req.url === '/items' && req.method ===
'POST') {
    let body = '';
    req.on('data', chunk => body += chunk);
    req.on('end', () => {
      const newItem = JSON.parse(body);
      items.push(newItem);
      res.writeHead(201, { 'Content-Type':
'application/json' });
      res.end(JSON.stringify(newItem));
    });
  } else {
    res.writeHead(404);
```

```
      res.end("Not Found");
  }
});
server.listen(3001, () => console.log("API
POST at http://localhost:3001"));
```

Outcome: Accepts JSON via POST, stores in `items`.

Exercise 9.3: GET and POST Combined

```
// apiGetPost.js
const http = require('http');
let users = [];
const server = http.createServer((req, res)
=> {
  if (req.url === '/users' && req.method ===
'GET') {
    res.writeHead(200, { 'Content-Type':
'application/json' });
    res.end(JSON.stringify(users));
  } else if (req.url === '/users' &&
req.method === 'POST') {
    let body = '';
    req.on('data', chunk => body += chunk);
    req.on('end', () => {
      const user = JSON.parse(body);
      user.id = users.length + 1;
      users.push(user);
      res.writeHead(201, { 'Content-Type':
'application/json' });
      res.end(JSON.stringify(user));
    });
  } else {
    res.writeHead(404);
    res.end("Not Found");
```

```
  }
});
server.listen(3002, () => console.log("Users
API at http://localhost:3002"));
```

Outcome: Store and retrieve user data in an in-memory array.

Exercise 9.4: Query String Filtering

```
// apiQueryFilter.js
const http = require('http');
const url = require('url');
const products = [
  { id: 1, name: "Pen" },
  { id: 2, name: "Pencil" },
  { id: 3, name: "Eraser" },
];
const server = http.createServer((req, res)
=> {
  const parsed = url.parse(req.url, true);
  if (parsed.pathname === '/products' &&
req.method === 'GET') {
    const search = (parsed.query.search ||
"").toLowerCase();
    const filtered = products.filter(p =>
p.name.toLowerCase().includes(search));
    res.writeHead(200, { 'Content-Type':
'application/json' });
    res.end(JSON.stringify(filtered));
  } else {
    res.writeHead(404);
    res.end();
  }
});
```

```
server.listen(3003, () =>
console.log("Products API at
http://localhost:3003"));
```

Outcome: Example: `GET /products?search=pen`.

Exercise 9.5: Return Error JSON for Missing Field

```javascript
// apiValidation.js
const http = require('http');
const server = http.createServer((req, res)
=> {
  if (req.url === '/items' && req.method ===
'POST') {
    let body = '';
    req.on('data', chunk => body += chunk);
    req.on('end', () => {
      const data = JSON.parse(body);
      if (!data.name) {
        res.writeHead(400, { 'Content-Type':
'application/json' });
        return res.end(JSON.stringify({
error: "Name is required" }));
      }
      res.writeHead(201, { 'Content-Type':
'application/json' });
      res.end(JSON.stringify({ status:
"Created", item: data }));
    });
  } else {
    res.writeHead(404).end();
  }
});
```

```
server.listen(3004, () =>
console.log("Validation API at
http://localhost:3004"));
```

Outcome: Returns 400 if name field is missing in the JSON body.

Exercise 9.6: Logging API Requests to File

```
// apiLogFile.js
const http = require('http');
const fs = require('fs');
const server = http.createServer((req, res)
=> {
  const logLine = `${new
Date().toISOString()} - ${req.method}
${req.url}\n`;
  fs.appendFile('api_requests.log', logLine,
err => {
    if (err) console.error("Log error:",
err);
  });
  res.writeHead(200);
  res.end("Request logged");
});
server.listen(3005, () =>
console.log("Logging API at
http://localhost:3005"));
```

Outcome: Each request is logged to api_requests.log.

Exercise 9.7: Minimal CORS Header Example

```
// apiCors.js
const http = require('http');
```

```
const server = http.createServer((req, res)
=> {
  // Very minimal CORS handling
  res.setHeader('Access-Control-Allow-
Origin', '*');
  if (req.url === '/data' && req.method ===
'GET') {
    const data = { msg: "Hello with CORS" };
    res.writeHead(200, { 'Content-Type':
'application/json' });
    res.end(JSON.stringify(data));
  } else {
    res.writeHead(404).end();
  }
});
server.listen(3006, () => console.log("CORS
API at http://localhost:3006"));
```

Outcome: Allows cross-origin GET from the browser fetch.

Exercise 9.8: Returning 404 for Unknown Paths

```
// api404.js
const http = require('http');
const server = http.createServer((req, res)
=> {
  if (req.url === '/hello' && req.method ===
'GET') {
    res.writeHead(200, { 'Content-Type':
'text/plain' });
    res.end("Hello!");
  } else {
    res.writeHead(404, { 'Content-Type':
'text/plain' });
    res.end("Not Found");
  }
```

```
});
server.listen(3007, () => console.log("404
API at http://localhost:3007"));
```

Outcome: All other routes get 404.

Exercise 9.9: Testing with Postman (Setup)

Objective: No code, but steps:

1. **Run** a server from previous exercise (e.g.,
   apiGetPost.js).
2. **Open** Postman, create a GET request to
   http://localhost:3002/users.
3. **Send** a POST request with JSON body.
   Outcome: Confirm your API logic.

Exercise 9.10: Testing with fetch in Browser

```
// fetchDemo.js
// (Not a server file, just an example usage
in the browser console):
/*
fetch('http://localhost:3002/users')
  .then(res => res.json())
  .then(data => console.log("User list:",
data));
fetch('http://localhost:3002/users', {
  method: 'POST',
  headers: { 'Content-Type':
'application/json' },
  body: JSON.stringify({ name: "Charlie" })
})
.then(res => res.json())
```

```
.then(data => console.log("New user:",
data));
*/
console.log("See comment for fetch usage in
the browser.");
```

Outcome: Illustrates how to test your Node API from client-side fetch requests.

Section 10: Next Steps and Learning Resources

These exercises encourage exploring Express.js, databases, testing, and real project expansions.

Exercise 10.1: Basic Express Server

```
// expressServer.js
const express = require('express');
const app = express();
app.get('/', (req, res) => {
  res.send("Hello from Express!");
});
app.listen(4000, () => {
  console.log("Express server at
http://localhost:4000");
});
```

Outcome: Start bridging from raw `http` to a framework-based approach.

Exercise 10.2: Express Middleware Example

```
// expressMiddleware.js
const express = require('express');
```

```
const app = express();
// Logger middleware
app.use((req, res, next) => {
  console.log(`Logged ${req.method}
${req.url}`);
  next();
});
app.get('/', (req, res) => {
  res.send("Middleware test");
});
app.listen(4001, () =>
console.log("Middleware server at port
4001"));
```

Outcome: Logs each incoming request method and path.

Exercise 10.3: Mongoose Connection

```
// mongooseConnect.js
const mongoose = require('mongoose');
mongoose.connect('mongodb://127.0.0.1:27017/t
estdb')
  .then(() => {
    console.log("Connected to MongoDB!");
    process.exit(0);
  })
  .catch(err => console.error("Error:",
err));
```

Outcome: Confirms your environment can connect to a local or remote MongoDB.

Exercise 10.4: Express + Mongoose Model

```
// expressMongoose.js
```

```
const express = require('express');
const mongoose = require('mongoose');
mongoose.connect('mongodb://127.0.0.1:27017/u
serdb');
const UserSchema = new mongoose.Schema({
name: String });
const User = mongoose.model('User',
UserSchema);
const app = express();
app.use(express.json());
app.post('/users', async (req, res) => {
  const user = new User(req.body);
  const saved = await user.save();
  res.status(201).json(saved);
});
app.listen(4002, () =>
console.log("Express+Mongoose at port
4002"));
```

Outcome: Simple endpoint to create a user in MongoDB.

Exercise 10.5: Building a To-Do List (Plan)

Objective: Outline your to-do project:

1. **Model**: fields for text, completed, date.
2. **Endpoints**: GET, POST, PUT/PATCH, DELETE.
3. **Storage**: Start with in-memory, then move to MongoDB.

Outcome: Roadmap for a bigger practice project.

Exercise 10.6: Creating a Random Joke Generator

```
// jokeGenerator.js
```

```javascript
const express = require('express');
const app = express();
const jokes = [
  "I'm reading a book about anti-gravity.
It's impossible to put down!",
  "Did you hear about the mathematician who's
afraid of negative numbers?",
  "Why do we tell actors to 'break a leg'?
Because every play has a cast."
];
app.get('/joke', (req, res) => {
  const randIndex = Math.floor(Math.random()
* jokes.length);
  res.json({ joke: jokes[randIndex] });
});
app.listen(4003, () => console.log("Joke
generator at port 4003"));
```

Outcome: Provides a random joke in JSON.

Exercise 10.7: Basic Unit Test with Jest (or Mocha)

```javascript
// sum.js
function sum(a, b) {
  return a + b;
}
module.exports = sum;
// sum.test.js (using Jest)
const sum = require('./sum');
test('adds 2 + 3 = 5', () => {
  expect(sum(2, 3)).toBe(5);
});
```

Outcome: Basic testing flow for Node. Configure "test":
"jest" in package.json.

Exercise 10.8: Setting Up ESLint

Install:

```
npm install --save-dev eslint
```
Initialize:

```
npx eslint --init
```

Outcome: Lint your Node.js code for style/quality checks.

Exercise 10.9: Building a Docker Image (Optional)

Objective: Show Node + Docker minimal example.

```
# Dockerfile
FROM node:14
WORKDIR /app
COPY package*.json ./
RUN npm install
COPY . .
CMD ["node", "index.js"]
```

Outcome: Containerize your Node app.

Exercise 10.10: Investigating Node Advanced Topics

Objective: Explore topics like clustering, worker threads, or load balancing (conceptual exercise).

1. **Read** Node.js docs on `cluster` or `worker_threads`.

Try a minimal cluster script:

```
// clusterDemo.js
```

```
// (Optional advanced exercise for multi-
process Node)
```

Outcome: Starting to learn advanced scaling approaches.

Closing Thoughts

You've engaged with Node.js from basic setup through more advanced topics like asynchronous programming, file management, package usage, server creation, building APIs, and continuing your journey with frameworks and databases. Adapt the exercises to build meaningful projects, experiment, and solidify your Node.js expertise.

Conclusion

Congratulations on completing **Node.js Made Simple: Hands-On Exercises for Node.js Beginners**! By working through the chapters and exercises in this book, you've taken a significant step toward mastering Node.js and server-side programming.

You've learned to:

- Build servers and APIs using Node.js's powerful core modules.
- Manage dependencies and packages with npm.
- Work with asynchronous programming and JavaScript promises.
- Create real-world projects that showcase Node.js's capabilities.

This book wasn't just about learning the theory—it was about rolling up your sleeves and coding. You've not only gained foundational knowledge of Node.js but also practical experience that prepares you to tackle real-world challenges.

Where to Go From Here

Your journey with Node.js doesn't stop here. Use the knowledge and skills you've gained to:

1. **Build Your Own Projects:** Start creating applications that solve problems you care about. Whether it's a simple API or a more complex application, the best way to solidify your skills is by building.
2. **Dive Deeper Into Node.js:** Explore more advanced topics like clustering, streams, performance optimization, and integrating with databases.
3. **Experiment with Frameworks:** Take your Node.js skills further by learning frameworks like Express.js or Nest.js, which simplify the process of building robust, scalable applications.
4. **Contribute to Open Source:** Join the Node.js community by contributing to open-source projects. This is a great way to learn, grow, and connect with other developers.
5. **Stay Curious:** The tech landscape evolves quickly. Keep learning, exploring, and experimenting with new tools and libraries in the Node.js ecosystem.

Thank You

Thank you for choosing this book to begin your Node.js journey. Your dedication to learning and improving is commendable. Remember, every great developer was once a beginner — what sets them apart is their willingness to keep growing.

About the Author

Laurence Lars Svekis is a renowned web developer, educator, and best-selling author, celebrated for his expertise in Node.js and server-side development. With over two decades of hands-on experience, Laurence has dedicated his career to making programming accessible, practical, and engaging for developers at all levels.

Laurence is a passionate advocate of Node.js as a transformative technology for modern web development. By combining JavaScript's versatility with Node.js's powerful runtime, he has helped countless developers unlock the potential of creating fast, scalable, and efficient server-side applications. Laurence's focus on real-world applications, practical problem-solving, and clean, modular code ensures that his teachings resonate with developers who aim to build solutions that are not only functional but also maintainable.

Having taught over one million students globally through his books, courses, and live presentations, Laurence is known for his interactive teaching style, which emphasizes hands-on learning. His step-by-step approach breaks down complex Node.js concepts — such as creating HTTP servers, working with APIs, managing asynchronous operations, and using npm — into digestible, actionable lessons. With Laurence as a guide, learners can quickly move from the basics of Node.js to building full-fledged applications.

In addition to being an educator, Laurence is a committed contributor to the Node.js community. He regularly shares insights, resources, and tools to help developers stay up-to-date with the ever-evolving Node.js ecosystem. His dedication to fostering collaboration and innovation has made him a respected figure in the developer community.

Laurence's ability to demystify Node.js has made him a trusted resource for beginners and experienced developers alike. Whether you're starting your journey with Node.js or looking to refine your skills, Laurence's practical approach ensures you'll gain the knowledge and confidence to succeed.

To discover more of Laurence's work, explore free Node.js resources, or stay informed about his latest projects, visit **BaseScripts.com**. Laurence's commitment to empowering developers continues to inspire and shape the future of server-side programming.

Related Titles

Practical Elements of Safety
Proceedings of the Twelfth Safety-critical Systems Symposium, Birmingham, UK, 2004
Redmill and Anderson (Eds)
1-85233-800-8

Constituents of Modern System-safety Thinking
Proceedings of the Thirteenth Safety-critical Systems Symposium, Southampton, UK, 2005
Redmill and Anderson (Eds)
1-85233-952-7

Developments in Risk-based Approaches to Safety
Proceedings of the Fourteenth Safety-critical Systems Symposium, Bristol, UK, 2006
Redmill and Anderson (Eds)
1-84628-333-7

The Safety of Systems
Proceedings of the Fifteenth Safety-critical Systems Symposium, Bristol, UK, 2007
Redmill and Anderson (Eds)
978-1-84628-805-0

Improvements in System Safety
Proceedings of the Sixteenth Safety-critical Systems Symposium, Bristol, UK, 2008
Redmill and Anderson (Eds)
978-1-84800-099-5

Safety-Critical Systems: Problems, Process and Practice
Proceedings of the Seventeenth Safety-critical Systems Symposium, Brighton, UK, 2009
Dale and Anderson (Eds)
978-1-84882-348-8

Making Systems Safer
Proceedings of the Eighteenth Safety-critical Systems Symposium, Bristol, UK, 2010
Dale and Anderson (Eds)
978-1-84996-085-4

Advances in Systems Safety
Proceedings of the Nineteenth Safety-critical Systems Symposium, Southampton, UK, 2011
Dale and Anderson (Eds)
978-0-85729-132-5

Achieving Systems Safety
Proceedings of the Twentieth Safety-critical Systems Symposium, Bristol, UK, 2012
Dale and Anderson (Eds)
978-1-4471-2493-1

Assuring the Safety of Systems
Proceedings of the Twenty-first Safety-critical Systems Symposium, Bristol, UK, 2013
Dale and Anderson (Eds)
978-1481018647